The 3 Estaites

To
John Carnegie

David Lindsay's

The 3 Estaites

The Millennium version by
Alan Spence

Edinburgh University Press

Caution

Amateur performances by schools and colleges in Scotland for assessment and educational purposes are authorised. Applications for public performance by amateurs or professionals must be addressed to Curtis Brown Ltd, 37 Queensferry Street, Edinburgh EH2 4QS (telephone 0131 225 1286).

No public performances may be given unless a licence has been obtained. Applications should be made in writing before rehearsals begin.

© Alan Spence, 2002

Edinburgh University Press Ltd
22 George Square, Edinburgh

First published by Learning and Teaching Scotland in 2002

Printed and bound in Great Britain by
The Cromwell Press Ltd, Trowbridge, Wilts

A CIP Record for this book is available from the British Library

ISBN 0 7486 1746 9 (paperback)

The right of Alan Spence to be identified as author of this work has been asserted accordance with the Copyright, Designs and Patents Act 1988.

The publishers acknowledge financial assistance in the publication of this volume from 2000 & 3 ESTAITES with funds originally derived from the Millennium Festival Fund.

Contents

Part Two

Note

Although divided into individual scenes for convenience of reference, the action in each of the two parts of the play is continuous.

Introduction
by Angus Calder

Ane Pleasant Satyre of the Thrie Estaites is the earliest Scottish play to have survived. It is surely the greatest Scottish play. It is also a European masterpiece. Lindsay's diplomatic missions for his master James V had taken him to London, to the court of the Holy Roman Emperor Charles V in Brussels, and above all to Paris. The *Satyre* shows knowledge of drama in France. It makes close and accurate reference to European politics, as well as to the religious controversies which were sweeping the continent. But it puts these together with the daily life of Lowland Scotland, the stench of the streets and the crack in the pubs. When Deceit in this play flatters King Humanity, the range of Lindsay's imagination is delightfully displayed. Alan Spence's new version captures it exactly:

> Sir, I ken by your physiognomy,
> You shall conquer, I clearly see,
> Gdansk and Germany and land of the Dane,
> Castlemilk and castles in Spain.
> You shall have at your governance
> Renfrew and aw the land of France,
> Rutherglen and the town of Rome,
> Corstorphine and all Christendom!

Lindsay was probably born around 1486. He died in 1555. That was a long life by the standards of his time. During it, he became one of the famous men of his native Fife. As a courtier with a known gift for writing verse and producing pageants, he may well have been the author of an 'interlude' (short play) performed indoors before James V at Linlithgow Palace in January 1540 which, as we know from a single report, had one or two features in common with the *Satyre*. It is absolutely certain that on 7th June 1552, this veteran who had set up entertainments for royalty provided the people of the small Fife town of Cupar near his big house at the Mount with a most astonishing outdoor spectacle – a play with 54 named parts for actors (if one includes its 'Proclamation'), full of broad humour and pantomime-like farce, but dealing with dangerous topical issues. The *Satyre* hits out at corruption and hypocrisy in the church, denounces oppression of the poor, and calls for social 'reformation' in the interests of the 'Commonweal'. A young king is rescued from idle sexual dalliance and false counsellors by Divine Correction – an emissary from God – and they preside over a Parliament summoned to enact just laws, where basic Christian tenets and values are affirmed.

In the days before newspapers (let alone TV and radio), there were two ways you could spread publicity. Most people went to church, where the parson could make announcements. Or you could send out a town crier through the streets to make a 'Proclamation'. Lindsay did more to publicise his play. He provided a kind of 'trailer', a comic sketch involving an old man, his young wife, a braggart coward and a cunning 'Fool'. This trailer anticipates, not the big themes of the play just mentioned, but several of its comic scenes. It says: 'Come and have fun'.

Summoned thus to Castle Hill in Cupar, people would have gathered on what was then called a 'playfield'. We can imagine the atmosphere of a big fair or festival, embracing all levels of society. Gentry in the audience would have had seats, but ordinary women, men and children would have promenaded, stood, sprawled or squatted as they heard 'Johne the Common-weill' speak up for them. There would have been hawkers of cloths and trinkets as well as vendors of food and drink. On the fringes, entertainers such as jugglers would have practised the popular arts of the day.

We can reconstruct the staging from Lindsay's stage directions. Spectators were divided from actors by a stream, the Lady Burn.

Parts of Castle Hill would have been fenced off. Inside the fence, the audience would have seen King Humanity's throne, a chamber into which the king could retire, a pulpit for sermons, a table and chairs. Stocks and gallows might have been inside or outside.

We can only guess who the actors were. Some must surely have been professional entertainers – minstrels and Fools (comedians). Most must have been amateurs from inside and outside Cupar. But some of these might well have been experienced, even outstanding, actors, who had featured in the so-called 'Robin Hood' plays which celebrated the arrival of summer or who had acted in serious religious dramas which craftsmen's guilds performed, traditionally at the Feast of Corpus Christi, or in 'clerks' plays' put on at the neighbouring University of St Andrews. There are big parts in Lindsay's very long play and he must have known and sought out people who could carry them off well.

Why did he go to the enormous trouble involved in writing and producing his *Satyre*? Again, we can only guess. It is possible that a festival in Cupar was already on the agenda when he offered to give it this focus. He may have invited friends and acquaintances who shared his deep concern about the state of church and society to come from all over Fife and farther afield, making the event in part a kind of political rally. One can imagine local people who had thrown themselves with gusto into making costumes, as happens in carnivals and other festivals in various parts of the world today, seeing the results with pride and glee. One can imagine general relaxation when Folly appeared at last, after some very heavy discussion of politics and religion. There was to be one more performance of the *Satyre*, presumably with a modified script, in front of the Regent, Mary of Guise (mother of Mary Queen of Scots), and much of the nobility. This took place on the Greenside playfield beside Calton Hill in Edinburgh, probably on 12th August 1554.

The play's serious points would have been reinforced by the presence of the actual ruler of the country.

Then, for nearly four centuries, the *Satyre* was never performed. Published in Edinburgh in 1602 and in London two years later, it would be read as largely a late-medieval morality play, in which characters with abstract nouns for names acted out an allegory presenting high religious and philosophical considerations. Otherwise, it drew on a French model, the *Sottie*, in which Fools played a central role. It was out of date in the new age of Shakespearian drama. Through the seventeenth century, religious and social controversy took new and more complex forms, so Lindsay would have seemed naive. In the eighteenth century, the idea of 'community theatre', which Lindsay had promoted on such a huge scale, was unthinkable. 'Enlightened' taste preferred classical theatre or sophisticated drawing-room comedies. Many members of the now established presbyterian church of Scotland thought theatre of any kind was wicked. As for the nineteenth century, Lindsay's genial acceptance of sexuality and constant reference to low bodily functions were the last things Victorians could have tolerated. Indeed, for most of the twentieth century, a great deal of his language would have been banned from stage, radio and TV. Even in 1948, when the Estates at last marched on stage backwards again at the Edinburgh Festival, Robert Kemp's fine adaptation could not be as broad and merry in its language as this new one by Alan Spence.

That 1948 revival was directed by a very remarkable man, Tyrone Guthrie, one of the most original and influential figures in twentieth-century theatre. He recreated the idea of a 'thrust stage', familiar to the ancient Greeks and to Shakespeare, where the audience sit on three sides of a performance, in contrast with the standard 'proscenium arch' mode, where the audience are in one space and the actors are in another. He found a richly appropriate space for the *Satyre* – the Church of Scotland Assembly Hall on the Mound. (Already the scene of the debates of the annual General Assembly of the Kirk, in 1999 it would become the temporary home of the new Scottish Parliament.) Here Guthrie could build a stage in the centre. The audience watched from pew-like seating on three sides.

Kemp's version modernised Lindsay's text and, of necessity, cut it very heavily. The original runs to 4,630 lines. (When it was given its second outing in Edinburgh in 1554, this much grander occasion went on from 9am to 6pm.) Kemp tried to rewrite Lindsay's language only where it was obscure, but he left out great swathes of the original text, particularly passages dealing with law and religious doctrine. His adaptation was a huge success in 1948 and has been revived at the Festival, with equal popularity, several times. (A different adaptation, by Tom Wright, was used in 1973 – then Kemp's returned.) The best Scottish actors have taken part in the *Satyre* and people from all over the world have enjoyed it.

In 2000 the *Satyre* returned to Cupar for the first time in nearly four and a half centuries. This new production aimed to celebrate the Millennium, and also the rebirth of Scotland's Parliament the year before – giving Lindsay's play fresh resonance.

Conditions were very different from those of 1552. Cupar, though still not very large, has expanded over and beyond its old playfield. On the site now called 'Castlehill', there is no castle and really no hill, just a courtyard in front of an agreeable Georgian building. It normally serves as a conveniently central car park. The new open-air production in this space was mounted by a specially formed company, 2000 & 3 ESTAITES, which had raised money for the project from the Millennium Festival Fund, Fife Council and various other sources. The Scottish Community Drama Association had given very enthusiastic support. The company's Artistic Director, John Carnegie, had assembled and rehearsed a cast of four professional performers and nearly thirty enthusiastic amateurs from the East of Scotland drawn in through the SCDA or individually. This deliberately paralleled the probable mix of Lindsay's original cast.

A new acting version was commissioned from Alan Spence. For all its merits, Kemp's version was the product of a staider period in Scottish culture. In particular, the literary use of 'Scots language' is no longer the preserve of nostalgic pedants. Younger generations of singers, novelists, playwrights, poets and comedians have reproduced and extended the vigour of actual everyday speech, which is what the new version captures. Spence restores a number of passages from Lindsay's original which Kemp omitted – above all, the crucially significant finale in which Folly carries all before him. But, since he has trimmed some of the more repetitive sections and speeches, his version takes slightly less time than Kemp's. It is 'racier' in two different senses of the word.

The new Cupar production had been 'trailed' in two ways. Parts of the new adaptation, still in draft, had been acted by a village drama group in Ayrshire and by three youth theatre groups elsewhere in Scotland. This was an important part of the whole project – to encourage as many performances of Lindsay in as many places as possible, and also to test out the text prior to final revision for the Cupar show. And, in the weeks prior to the opening of the Millennium production on 2nd July, unannounced performances of the Proclamation erupted in high streets and shopping centres across the East of Scotland. Surprised and delighted citizens were distracted from their messages and many were thus lured to Cupar, where nine performances of *The 3 Estaites* took place in front of very satisfactory audiences seated on scaffolding round three sides of the courtyard or promenading in the thick of the action. The reviews were good. Elaine Robertson's costumes were particularly vivid. Gordon Dougall's music was infectiously sparky. The sheer gusto of the acting was delightful. Lindsay's masterpiece is still funny and still moving.

Why does the *Pleasant Satyre of the Thrie Estaites* still work so well, coming as it does from a very particular moment in time which might seem utterly remote from our own? In 1552 Scotland was just eight years away from its Protestant Reformation, which Lindsay would not live to see. As he wrote, a reformed Catholic church was perhaps a likelier possibility. One Catholic, Mary of Guise, ruled in Scotland. Another, Mary Tudor, would soon arrive on the throne of England, reversing the Protestant Reformation there. The leaders of Scottish Roman Catholicism wanted to purify their church so as to counter the kind of criticism we hear in the *Satyre*.

But the ideas of Luther and Calvin had strong appeal for growing numbers of literate Scots laymen – anxious to read the Bible in English and receive the word of God direct. Such people despised the ignorance of many, perhaps most, parish priests. There were other causes of strong anti-clerical feeling. Priests, as we learn from the Poor Man in the *Satyre*, exacted teinds to support themselves – a tenth part of the produce of every parish. The church was a major landowner. Its recent greedy switch from leasing out land to the system of 'feu ferme' dispossessed about a third of its tenants who could not afford greatly increased dues. Even those who could, and thus got inheritable right to their land, might well be unsettled by the change.

The question of sexual laxity amongst clergy is complex. In the present new century, the issue of clerical celibacy has become extremely topical again, with many suggesting that the sinister occurrence of paedophilia among Catholic priests might be reduced if they were allowed to marry. Lindsay himself would have favoured permitting clergy to marry, but clearly despised the hypocrisy of bishops and others, committed by church rules to celibacy, who nevertheless kept concubines. At the end of the *Satyre*, the Prioress who is stripped of her clerical garb and found to be using sexy underwear is a splendid symbol of such hypocrisy.

But it must be stressed that this is not an anti-Catholic play. Its agenda is reform of a church which is still Catholic, reasserting basic, orthodox Christian doctrine. And Lindsay's concept of 'reformation' goes way beyond the church.

His play is about the duties of governors and the abuse and right use of power. That is why it still speaks to us in the days of a new Scottish Parliament. We have seen Dame Sensuality within living memory divert a king (Edward VIII) from his duty and topple more than one cabinet minister from office. At the end of the *Satyre*, that coarsely cynical fat cat, Bishop Spirituality, is unrepentant, but the leaders of the other two Estates, Temporality and Merchant, concur that justice for the poor is essential. It is the passionate plea for a just Scotland by Johne the Common-weill which dominates the key late scenes of the play.

'Johne' in Lindsay's original, 'Jane' in Alan Spence's adaptation. The other important character undergoing sex-change is Guid Counsel. This suits present-day notions of sexual equality – though it is worth pointing out that, even in 1552, Lindsay made two women, Verity and Chastity, heads of the church at the end.

What else has Alan Spence done that is fresh? He has brilliantly updated the play's topical allusions. Two examples . . . In the Proclamation, Lindsay's braggart coward is Fynlaw of the Fute Band – that is, a member of an infantry company – who boasts that he could have beaten the English at Pinkie in 1547 when, on the contrary, the Scots were thrashed. We don't fight wars against the English any more, except on sporting fields, so Finlay the Fitba Fan of the Tartan Army is Spence's very neat substitution. Secondly, you might think that when Folly declares to the Parliament:

> Now of my sermon I have made an end.
> To Billy Connolly I ye all commend . . .

this is a gratuitous improvisation. Not so. The original Lindsay text reads:

> Now of my sermon have I maid ane end:
> To Gilly-moubrand I yow all commend . . .

Gilly-moubrand was a Fool at the court of James V in Lindsay's own time there. As a stand-up comic, Connolly is a notable contemporary Fool. (He has also been close to certain younger royals in the present court.)

Lindsay's text included local jokes. Spence got a huge laugh from audiences in Cupar by changing a passage soon after Folly enters:

> DILIGENCE: Fond fuill, quhair hes thou bene sa lait?
> FOLY: Marie, command throw the Bony Gait . . .

Spence referred to a problem in that principal Cupar street which had made headlines in the local press in 2000:

> DILIGENCE: Daft fool, what's got ye in such a state?
> FOLLY: It's they traffic lights in the Bonnygate . . .

Granted the up-to-date, *local* character of Lindsay's original play, would it be sacrilegious if someone staging Spence's version were to make similar changes where possible . . . ?

Though most of Lindsay's text is closer to present-day speech in this island than most of Shakespeare, strange old Scots spellings and weird words found in the standard edition by Roderick Lyall

(Canongate Classics, 1989) may put many readers off. Spence gives his actors the parlance of us in pub and club (and at Hampden Park) today. If you can follow Irvine Welsh, you can grasp this version of Lindsay. But how can we justify changing the words of a great dramatist? Would people rewrite Shakespeare? (Well, it has been known . . .)

While there are some noble passages of poetry in the 1552 *Satyre*, and some pleasantly sensuous ones, Lindsay didn't write tight verse like Shakespeare. He swung from rhyme to rhyme loosely, with cheerful abandon and astonishing zest. He differentiated characters and situations by varying line length and rhythm. If you keep those, as Spence does, you preserve his generous spirit. Lindsay's a very serious man who nevertheless has a terrific sense of fun.

He also has an eye and an ear for character and situation which go way beyond the big English morality plays of his era. Despite their abstract names, his characters are wholly real people, which is why actors love this play so much. And what a varied bunch – from Divine Correction booming out his vituperations to Poor Man moaning out his sad tale and the craftsmen with their quarrelsome wives. Flattery bounces on stage after his distressing sea voyage with such jolly charm that we're not going to mind it when he alone of the three Vices escapes hanging at the end, any more than we object to Sensuality surging off to make fresh conquests in other kingdoms. It is a delicious moment when the previously sour little Prioress announces, with a dancing verse rhythm, that she's glad to be unfrocked and is going off to find a husband; a slightly astonishing one when Folly tells King Humanity that he's a Fool too, just like everyone else. I don't think that negates the serious work of Divine Correction through the Parliament or the triumph of Jane the Common-weil. The point is that we are all in Lindsay's vision fallible human beings – but we can be fun. Beyond conventions of Morality and *Sottie*, this is a national drama, expressing a comprehensive perspective of what Scotland is and what it might be – a land of justice, fellow-feeling and laughter.

May 2002

Original cast list

The first full performance of Sir David Lindsay's play was given on Castlehill in Cupar on 7th June 1552. This adaptation was commissioned by 2000 & 3 ESTAITES with the support of the Millennium Festival Fund. As part of the company's Millennium project, performances of parts of an earlier draft of this adaptation were given by The Dunlop Players, Borders Youth Theatre, Dunfermline Children's Heritage Theatre and Rothes Halls Youth Theatre during March to May 2000. 2000 & 3 ESTAITES first performed The Proclamation at the Mercat Cross in the High Street in Edinburgh and Ferguson Square in Cupar on 28th April 2000. The first full performance of this adaptation was given by 2000 & 3 ESTAITES on Castlehill in Cupar on 2nd July 2000 in the version printed here. In that performance, the cast (in order of speaking) were:

The Proclamation

DILIGENCE, a herald	John A. Sampson
COTTAR	Alan Redpath
MRS COTTAR	Fiona A. Hunter
FINLAY THE FITBA FAN	John K. Marshall
THE FOOL	David Hunter

The Play

DILIGENCE, a herald	John A. Sampson
KING HUMANITY	David Hunter
WANTONNESS, courtier to the King	Alastair Sim
CHILL-OOT, courtier to the King	Andrew Laughton
SANDY SOLACE, courtier to the King	Martin Butler

DAME SENSUALITY	**Gerda Stevenson**
HAMELINESS, handmaiden to Sensuality	**Fiona A. Hunter**
DANGER, handmaiden to Sensuality	**Yvonne Briglmen**
JANET, handmaiden to Sensuality	**Yvonne Cook**
GUID COUNSEL, a Virtue	**Anna Maciocia**
FLATTERY, a Vice who masquerades as 'Devotion'	**Alan Redpath**
FALSEHOOD, a Vice who masquerades as 'Sanity'	
	Matthew Burgess
DECEIT, a Vice who masquerades as 'Discretion'	**Robert Pattison**
VERITY, a Virtue	**Kate Potter**
THE BISHOP, head of the Spiritual Estaite	**Charles K. Gallacher**
THE PRIORESS, member of the Spiritual Estaite	**Catriona Joss**
THE PARSON, member of the Spiritual Estaite	**Robert Camron**
CHASTITY, a Virtue	**Catherine Beckley**
TEMPORALITY, head of the Estaite of Craftsmen	**John A. Gray**
MERCHANT, head of the Estaite of Merchants	**Esther Wood**
SOUTAR, a craftsman	**Gordon Dougall**
TAYLOR, a craftsman	**Alastair Ferguson-Smith**
JENNY TAYLOR	**Kirsty Kelly/Nghaire Gonnella**
MRS TAYLOR	**Margot Taylor**
MRS SOUTAR	**Irene Robb**
DIVINE CORRECTION'S VARLET	
	Danielle Corr/Donna Sutherland/Jennifer Boulton
DIVINE CORRECTION	**Michael Mackenzie**
THE POOR MAN	**Alastair Ferguson-Smith**
JANE THE COMMON-WEIL	**Gerda Stevenson**
FIRST SERGEANT	**Fiona Dingwall**
SECOND SERGEANT	**Fiona A. Hunter**
FOLLY	**Michael Mackenzie**

Directed by **John Carnegie**
Designed by **Elaine Robertson**
Music by **Gordon Dougall**

The 3 Estaites

The Proclamation

The Proclamation

(performed as a 'trailer' in the weeks before the play)

Diligence, a herald, comes on.

DILIGENCE: Guid people, hear what I have come to say!
Pin back yer lugs, I'll tell ye of our play.
I've got thegether wi a wheen o my best mates
Tae act a great play cried 'The Thrie Estaites'.
It's been around since 1552.
This summer we'll perform it just for you.
This is like a trailer, a 'coming attraction',
To give ye all a wee taste of the action!

Richt famous people, ye shall understand
How that a prince richt wise and vigilant
Is shortly for to come into this land
And purposes to hold a Parliament.
His Thrie Estaites thereto have made consent
In Cupar toon into their best array,
With support of the Lord omnipotent,
And thereto have affixed a certain day.

Fail not to be upon the Castlehill
Beside the place where we purpose to play.
With good strong wine your flagons see ye fill,
And hold yourself the merriest that ye may.
Be not displeased whatever we sing or say,
Though our material may be beyond the pale!
July the second's the first night of our play –
If you are there, forsooth we shall not fail!

COTTAR: *(Emerging from the audience)*
                I'll be there, pal, by God's grace,
                Though thousands can't get near the place,
                I'll be first at this fair!
                I'll drink a few pints in the toon
                Wi my good mates, then swagger doon,
                Nae problem, I'll be there!

MRS COTTAR: *(Taking Diligence's place on the stage)*
                Where have ye been, daft drunken loon?
                Blootered and bevvied in the toon?
                What time d'ye call this to come hame?

COTTAR: Ach give us peace, hen! In the name!
                Yon mannie bent my ear to say
                Some folk are coming wi a play.

MRS COTTAR: A play? That sounds the very thing for me.
                And you can bide at hame and mak the tea!

COTTAR: When you get steamin wi the drink,
                Beside you nane can stand for stink!
                So you should bide at hame that day,
                And let me go and see the play!

MRS COTTAR: That I will not! I'll skelp your lug!

COTTAR: See how she treats me, like a dug!

They move off. Enter Finlay the Fitba Fan.

FINLAY: Scot-land! Scot-land! Scot-land! Scotland!
There's nae man against me can stand
Fae Hampden to Wembley!
A pure heidbanger, mental, bammy,
I'm Finlay o the Tartan Army –
I'll mak your legs trembly!
When England stole three points frae us,
I fought a haill supporters' bus
And gave them a doing!
It was wan monumental claim,
I sent them homewards to think again
Aw hissing and booing!

He lies down. The Fool enters.

THE FOOL: Good God! By Him that wore the croon of thorn,
Yon's the biggest coward since God was born!
He loves himself and puts all others doon –
I ken him weil, a boastful braggart loon.
For aa his hardman fitba casual style,
Ye bark at him, the clown will run a mile!

Enter Cottar and his wife, both drunk, reconciled.

COTTAR: Come here, my wife, I must lie down and sleep,
And in my arms my company you'll keep.
But first, my love, I'll have to shut this lock
And hide the key – I hope that's no a shock.

He locks his wife in a chastity belt and lays the key under his head.
He lies down to sleep while his wife sits up beside him.

FINLAY: *(Wakes up, sees Cottar and his wife)*
I am sae hardy, sturdy, strang and stout
That out of Hell the Deil I dare ding out!
(To Mrs Cottar)
Hullaw there darlin! Lusty lady bright!
I'd love to lie beside you there all night!

She gives him two fingers, sends him packing. The Fool watches him go, approaches her.

THE FOOL: *(Indicating his enormous phallus)*
So long as this can stir and stand,
It shall be aye at your command!
Is it no the best that ye ever saw?

MRS COTTAR: Now welcome to me above them aa!

THE FOOL: *(Seeing the belt)*
Thinks he not shame and black disgrace
To put a lock on that sweet place?

MRS COTTAR: But see if you can get me freed –
Steal the key frae under his heid!

THE FOOL: That shall I do, without a doubt!
Let's see if I can get it out.
Right! Here's the key. Do what ye will!

MRS COTTAR: Now then, let us go play our fill!

They lock the sleeping husband in the chastity belt and then run off. Finlay is swaggering about.

FINLAY: O flower of Scotland! When will we see...
There's naebody can stand up to me.
I'll kick the shit out any foe.
Here we go! Here we go...!

Cottar is woken by the noise.

COTTAR: In the name of God, who makes that row?
(Sits up, sees his wife's gone)
My trouble and strife, where are ye now?
Where have ye gone, my ain sweet thing,
Love of my life, my wee darling?
(Feels around for the key)
Aw naw! Jings! Crivvens! Michty me!
I've went and lost the bloody key!
Now she'll call me a feckless jock –
To have her I must break the lock!

MRS COTTAR: *(Coming back on carrying a shirt)*
What now, good man, why dae ye rave?

COTTAR: Nothing, my heart, but you I crave.
Have you been busy in the kitchen?

MRS COTTAR: For you a new shirt I've been stitching,
Of Flemish cotton, baith white and tough –
Let's see if it is wide enough.

She pulls the shirt over his head and the Fool replaces the key and takes off.

COTTAR: It fits me very well, my heart.
Aw darling, let us never part!
Ye are the fairest of the flock.
(amorous)
Where is the key, now, for this lock?

MRS COTTAR: Ye rave, guid man! Your brains are deid!
I saw you lay it under your heid!

COTTAR: In the name of God now, that is true!
That I suspected you, sair I rue.
I doubt there is nae man in Fife
That ever had sae guid a wife.
My ain sweetheart, I think it best
That we lie doon and tak some rest!

They snuggle down.

FINLAY: *(Coming back on)*
It's terrible, this place is shite!
There's naebody for me to fight.
If big Goliath came oot that door,
I'd stick the heid on him for sure!
And Hercules? I'd break his bones.
I'd even tackle Vinnie Jones!

THE FOOL: *(Sneaking up behind him)*
Boo!

FINLAY: In the name of God! What's that smell?
I do believe I've shat mysel!
I've never met a fiercer foe –
For God's sake, Jimmy, let me go!

The Fool kicks him up the backside, laughs as he runs off.

DILIGENCE: As for this day, I have nae mair to say noo.
Make sure ye come and see our play, I pray you.
Oh, and use the toilets first for, by Hell's bells,
I guarantee...

ALL FIVE: ...we'll make ye wet yersels!

The 3 Estaites

Part One

Scene 1: Prologue

Fanfare. Enter Diligence, the herald, accompanied by most of the rest of the cast.

ALL: The Faither and founder of faith and felicity,
That your fashion formed to his similitude,
And His Son, our Saviour, our shield in necessity,
That saved you from all harm, ransomed on the Rood,
Redeeming His prisoners with His precious blood,
The Haily Gaist, governor and grounder of grace,
Of wisdom and welfare both fountain and flood,
Save you all that sit and stand here in this place,
And shield you from sin,
And with His spirit you inspire.
Till we have shown our desire,
Silence, sovereigns, we require,
For now we begin!

The Estaites of Spirituality (Bishop, Prioress and Parson), Temporality and the Merchants take their places.

DILIGENCE: Tak tent, my friends, and haud yer wheesht!
For I stand before you, not as a priesht,
But messenger from a richt royal king,
Who for mony a year has been absent, travelling.
If you want to know his name, it's King Humanity,
And he bade me tell you this with great alacrity,
That he intends to mak here an appearance
With a triumphant awesome ordinance,

Wearing a crown, a sceptre in his hand,
Tempered with mercy when penitence appears.
Humanity's been owre long sleeping in this land,
Whereby misrule has reigned here mony years
And innocents have been beset with fears
By false reporters of this nation
Though young oppressors learn from elder peers,
Be now assured of reformation.

And here by open proclamation,
I warn in the name of his magnificence,
The Thrie Estaites of this nation,
That they appear with all due diligence
And to his Grace mak their obedience.
So first I warn the Spirituality,
And, Merchants, spare ye no expense,
But gather here with Temporality.

And I beseech you, famous auditors,
Convened here in this congregation,
To be patient for the space of a few hours,
Till you have heard our short narration.
Also we mak you supplication
That no man tak our words into disdain,
Although you hear by declamation
The Common-Weil richt piteously complain.

Richt so the virtuous Lady Verity
Will mak lament and hing her puir heid doon
And for the truth she will imprisoned be
And banished a lang time oot o this toon.
And Chastity will suffer sair rejection.
For she will get nae ludging in this land
Until the heavenly Divine Correction
Meet wi the King and Commons hand for hand.

Prudent people, pray silence the tones
On all yer watches and mobile phones
And dinnae tak photos or we'll break yer bones!
Please don't disturb our play.
And so, till all our rhymes be rung,
And all our tuneless songs be sung,
Let every man keep weel ane tongue
And every woman tway!

Scene 2: The King and his Courtiers

The King is left onstage with Wantonness and Chill-oot.

KING HUMANITY: O Lord of Lords and King of Kings severe,
Omnipotent of power, prince without peer,
Unmade maker, who created matter,
Made heaven and earth, made fire, air and watter,
Send me thy grace, with peace perpetual,
And bring my soul to joy angelical.
Since thou hast given me dominion
And rule of people subject to my care,
Tak pity, Lord, on me thy merest minion,
And help me thole the burdens I maun bear.

I thee request, who rent was on the Rood,
Defend me too from deeds of dark defame,
That my people report of me nocht but good.
Be thou my safeguard from all sin and shame.
I know my days endure but as a dream,
Therefore, my Lord, I heartily thee exhort
To give me grace to use my diadem
To thy pleasure and to my own comfort.

WANTONNESS: My sovereign lord, prince without peer,
What gars you mak sic dreary cheer?
Be blyth so long as you are here
And pass time with pleasure.
For as long lives the merry man
As the sorry. Do what he can,
Him wi the soor face I shall ban
That does you displeasure.
As long as guid Chill-oot and me
Remain here in your company,
Your Grace shall live richt merrily,
Wi charm and cheer maist choice.
So long as you have us, be sure,
Your Grace shall never lack pleasure.
And if Solace were here I you assure,
With us he would rejoice.

CHILL-OOT: Good brother of mine, where is Solace,
The mirror of all merriness?
It maks me marvel, by the Mass,
He tarries there so lang.
I wonder why he's up and went,
And bides awa withoot consent,
I doubt there's some impediment
Prevents him for tae gang.

WANTONNESS: I left Solace, that same great loon,
Drinking somewhere in the toon.
Throwing away his last half-croon –
He hasnae ony mair.
Then he said he would gang see
Fair Lady Sensuality,
The bright pearl of all beauty
And finest features fair.

Sandy Solace enters.

CHILL-OOT: By God, I see him here at last,
As if he's been chased, running fast,
Glowering as if he was aghast,
Or frightened by a ghost!
No, he's mad drunk, that's the truth,
From slaking his insatiable drouth.
I can tell by his greasy mooth,
That he's been at a feast.

SOLACE: Now, who ever saw such a thrang?
                  I thought some said I had gone wrang.
                  If I had help, I would sing a sang
                  And make a richt merry noise!
                  I have such pleasure in my heart,
                  It makes me sing the treble part.
                  If some good fellow would fill the quart,
                  Then my heart would rejoice.
                  What is my name? Can ye no guess?
                  Sirs, d'ye no ken Sandy Solace?
                  They called my mother Bonnie Bess,
                  A most accommodating lass.
                  At twelve year old she learned her tricks –
                  Thanks be to God that men hae pricks –
                  Fathers I had five or six,
                  And that's the truth, no less.
                  When one was deid, she got another,
                  Never a man had such a mother.
                  Another father? That's nae bother!
                  Rich men as weel as poor,
                  She spared neither cook nor knight,
                  Had four and twenty in one night,
                  Left them bleary eyed, what a sight!
                  All worthy, weel-hung for sure!
                  You can ask, if you think I lie,
                  But here, have you seen the King come by?
                  He said he would, within short space
                  Of time come meet me at this place.

KING HUMANITY: My servant, Solace, what made you tarry?

SOLACE: I know not, Sir, by sweet Saint Mary.
            I must have been away wi the fairies!
            Or else I've been in a trance.
            Sir, I have seen, and this is sure,
            The fairest earthly creature
            That ever was formed by nature
            To make your senses dance.
            To look on her is great delight,
            With lips so red and cheeks so white,
            I would renounce all this world, quite,
            For to stand in her grace.
            She is wanton and she is wise,
            All dressed in the most stylish guise.
            It would mak your flesh uprise
            To look upon her face.

KING HUMANITY: Dear God! My friends, I think you are not wise
            To counsel me to break commandment
            Directed by the Prince of Paradise.
            Considering you know that my intent
            Is to remain to God obedient,
            Who does forbid men to be lecherous.
            If I do not, perchance I shall repent,
            Therefore I think your counsel odious.
            I have been a pure white page until
            This moment, ready for good and ill.

WANTONNESS: Do you believe that lechery be sin?
               No, not at all, Sir. Here's my reason why.
               First at the court of Rome you may begin,
               Which is the lighted lamp of lechery,
               Where cardinals and bishops generally
               Think to love the ladies a pleasant sport,
               And out of Rome have banished Chastity,
               Who with our prelates has no resort.

SOLACE: Sir, till you get a prudent Queen,
               I think your Majesty serene
               Should have a lusty lass maist keen
               To play you withal.
               For I know by your quality
               You want the gift of chastity.
               Fall to, in nomine Domini,
               This is my counsel.
               I speak, Sir, under protestation,
               So none at me take indignation,
               For all the prelates of this nation,
               For the most part,
               Think it no shame to have a whoor,
               And some of them have three or four,
               This is true, you may be sure.
               To each his ain tart.
               Sir, if you knew these 'holy orders'
               To play you would begin.
               Ask all the monks from here to the Borders
               If lechery be sin!

CHILL-OOT: Sir, send for Sandy Solace,
                Or else your minion Wantonness,
                And pray my lady Prioress
                The truth to declare,
                If it be sin to go oot whooring,
                Wi some lusty lass to hae a fling –
                The guid book says Examine a'thing,
                And nocht to spare.

Scene 3: The entrance of Sensuality

Dame Sensuality enters – accompanied by her three handmaidens.

SENSUALITY: Lovers awake! Behold the fiery sphere,
                Behold the natural daughter of Venus,
                Behold, lovers, this lusty lady clear,
                The fresh fountain of knights so amorous,
                Replete with joys, sweet and delicious.
                Whoever would mak to Venus observance
                In my mirthful chamber melodious,
                There shall they find all pastime and pleasance.
                Behold my heid, behold my gay attire,
                Behold my neck, lovely and lily-white,
                Behold my face, flaming as the fire,
                Behold my paps, perfect in your sight,
                To look on me gives lovers great delight,
                For so have all the kings in Christendom –
                To them I have shown pleasures infinite,
                Especially in the great court of Rome.
                One kiss from me is worth, in one morning,
                A million pound in gold to knight or king.
                Yet I'm so prone all my love to impart,

I let no lover pass with a sore heart.
Of my name would you know the verity,
For they call me Sensuality.
I think it best, before we move along,
To Dame Venus let us sing a song.

HAMELINESS: Let's not be tarrying,
But serve Venus dear,
We shall fall to and sing,
Sister Danger, come near!

DANGER: Sister, sing this song I cannot,
Without the help of good Friend-Janet.
Friend-Janet, come and tak a part!

JANET: That shall I do with all my heart!
You both should love me, is that not so?
I taught you everything you know,
In my chamber, you know fine where,
And now there's not a man you'll spare!

HAMELINESS: Friend-Janet, fie! You are to blame!
To speak foul words, hae you no shame?

JANET: These hundreds gathered here to see
Love laying just as much as me –
Might they get it privately.
But who begins the song, let's see!

ALL FOUR WOMEN: *(Singing)*
>Come, lads and lassies, listen tae the sang.
>Come, wi each other lie.
>Now is the moment, how can it be wrang?
>Now as the time gangs by.
>
>Join in the dance, we're only here a while.
>Flowers they bloom and die.
>Cling close thegether, mak each other smile.
>Now as the time gangs by.
>
>Come, lads and lassies, listen tae the sang.
>Come, wi each other lie.
>Now is the moment, how can it be wrang?
>Now as the time gangs by.
>
>Come, lads and lassies, come.
>Come, lads and lassies, come.

Scene 4: The King anticipates Sensuality

KING HUMANITY: Up, Wantonness, you sleep too long!
>I thought I heard a merry song.
>Now I command you, run along,
>See what this mirth might mean.

WANTONNESS: I trust, Sir, by the Trinity,
>That same is Sensuality.
>If it be so, soon shall I see
>That sovereign serene.

CHILL-OOT: She is so fair of countenance,
               And she can both play and dance,
               A perfect patron of pleasance,
               And pearl of pulchritude.
               Soft as silk is her white skin,
               Raven her hair, of lustrous sheen,
               My heart burns like a fire within,
               I swear it by the Rood.

SOLACE: What say you, Sir, are you content
               She comes here as if heaven-sent?
               What avails your kingdom, your rent
               And all of your great treasure,
               Unless you have a merry life
               And cast aside all stress and strife?
               As long as you have not a wife,
               Fall to and take your pleasure!

KING HUMANITY: Forsooth, I know not how it stands,
               My body has its own commands,
               I tremble in my feet and hands
               And burn as hot as fire.
               It seems that Cupid with his dart
               Has wounded me deep in the heart,
               My spirit will from my body part
               If I get not my desire.
               Pass on away with diligence,
               And bring her here to my presence.
               Spare not for travel nor expense,
               I care not for the cost.

Be on your way soon, Wantonness,
And tak with you Sandy Solace,
And bring that lady to this place,
Or else I shall be lost!
Commend me to that sweetest thing,
And give to her this precious ring,
And say I lie here languishing
Until she comes to save me.
With sighing sore I sit and grieve,
Till here forthwith her way she'll weave,
My heavy languor to relieve,
And from the dead to raise me.

WANTONNESS: Doubt ye not, Sir, that we will get her,
We shall be eager for to net her,
But faith, we would speed all the better
If our money bags were full.

SOLACE: Sir, let not sorrow in you sink,
But give us ducats for a drink,
And we shall never sleep a wink
Till we bring you this jewel.

KING HUMANITY: Now, sirs, win well your wage,
I pray you, speed you soon again.

WANTONNESS: We shall not spare for wind or rain
Till our work be done soon.
Farewell, for we are at the flight,
We shall be here before midnight,
Though we march with the moon.

Wantonness and Solace traverse the stage towards Sensuality.

Scene 5: The Courtiers' embassy to Sensuality

WANTONNESS: Pastime with pleasance and great prosperity,
                Be to you, Sovereign Sensuality!

SENSUALITY: Sirs, you are welcome. Where go you, east or west?

WANTONNESS: In faith, I think we have achieved our quest.

SENSUALITY: What is your name, that has a tongue sae merry?

WANTONNESS: I am Wantonness, the good King's Secretary.

SENSUALITY: What King is that, whose praises now you sing?

WANTONNESS: Humanity's this great and noble King,
                To you this day his heartfelt praise we bring.
                He sends you here a lustrous ruby ring,
                As token that above all creature,
                He has chosen you to be his paramour.
                He bade me say that he will surely die,
                Unless you will consent with him to lie.

SENSUALITY: How can I help the King, if he be sick?
                You know fine well that I am no medic.

SOLACE: Dear lady, though he may be sick, for sure
                Your lovely body is the very cure.
                One kiss of your sweet mouth in the morning
                To his sickness might be great comforting.
                And so he says this night he would be blessed
                If you would sup with him and be his guest.

SENSUALITY: I thank His Grace for his benevolence,
Good sirs, I shall be ready and at hand.
In me there shall be found no negligence,
Both day and night when his grace will demand.
Go on ahead, I'll follow by command.
I think right long to have of him a sight,
And I with Venus pledge to mak him stand
And in his arms I think to lie all night.

WANTONNESS: That shall be done, but before I must fly,
Your maid, Hameliness, pleases my eye.

SENSUALITY: She shall be at command, sir, when you will.
I trust she shall find you flinging your fill.

SOLACE: Now hey! For joy and mirth I dance!
Take up a gay gavotte fae France!
Am I not worthy to advance,
That am so good a page,
And so speedily can run,
To entice my maister into sin?
The fiend a penny he will win
From this his lucky marriage.
I rue already, by Saint Michael,
That I had not pierced her masel.
Forgive my bluntness, one and all,
Of love the King knows bugger all!

Scene 6: The Courtiers' return to the King

Wantonness and Solace return to the King.

WANTONNESS: *(To the King)*
Good morrow, Maister, by the Mass!

KING HUMANITY: Welcome my minion, Wantonness!
How have you fared in your travel?

WANTONNESS: Right well, by Him that harried Hell,
Your errand is well done.

KING HUMANITY: Then Wantonness, how well is me.
You have deserved both food and fee,
By Him that made the sun.
There is one thing, one doubt, I fear –
What shall I do when she comes near?
I never learned this craft so dear,
The lover's art.
Therefore you must teach me right here
How I should start.

WANTONNESS: To kiss and clap her, Sir, be not afraid.
She will not shrink though you kiss her down there
– she is no maid!
If you think that she is ashamed, then cover her eyes
With her dress, and hold her well, that's my advice.
Will you allow me, Sir, first to go to?
That way I can teach you what you should do.

KING HUMANITY: God forbid, Wantonness, that I give leave!
That you should even ask beggars belief.

WANTONNESS: Now, Sir, try as you please. I see her coming.
We're with you. Behave with gravity, my King.

Scene 7: Sensuality comes to the King

SENSUALITY: To Queen Venus, celestial majesty,
I give glory, honour, laud and reverence,
Who granted me such bounteous blissful beauty
That princes in my person take pleasance.
I mak one vow, with humble observance,
Richt reverently thy temple I will see
And mak due sacrifice to thy divinity.
To every state I'm so agreeable
That few or none refuses me at all –
Popes, patriarchs and prelates venerable,
Common people and princes temporal
Are subject all to me, Dame Sensual.
They sit here at my feet, both rich and poor.
So shall it be then, while the world endure.
And now my way I must advance,
To a prince of great puissance.
Whom young men has in governance.
Around him they revolve.

I am richt glad, I you assure,
This potent prince to take and cure,
Who is of lustiness the lure
And greatest of resolve.
O potent prince, renowned for pulchritude,
May the god Cupid preserve thee, by all guid,
And may Dame Venus keep thee in beatitude,
As I would she should keep my own heart's blood.

KING HUMANITY: Welcome to me, o peerless perfect beauty.
Welcome to me, thou who are sweeter than amber.
You have now stripped me bare of all misery.
Solace, convey this lady to my chamber!

SENSUALITY: I go to it with richt guid will.
Sir Wantonness, tarry you still.
And Hameliness, his cup you'll fill
And keep him company.

HAMELINESS: That shall I do without delay,
And he and I shall sport and play.

WANTONNESS: Now lady, pour my drink, I pray,
Fill in, for I am dry.
Your dame by now truly
Is using well her lips.
What say now you and I
Go join us at the hips?

HAMELINESS: Content am I, with richt guid will
Whenever you are ready,
All your pleasure to fulfil.

WANTONNESS: Now well said, by our Lady!
I'll keep my maister company
As long as I can bear.
If he be whistling wantonly,
We'll fling us on the flair!

Observed by Guid Counsel, they move into the chamber.

Scene 8: The entrance of Guid Counsel

GUID COUNSEL: Immortal God, most high magnificence,
Whose majesty no church can comprehend,
Must save you all that gives such audience
And grant you grace Him never to offend,
Who on the Cross did willingly ascend
And shed His precious blood on every side,
Whose pitious passion from danger you defend,
And is your gracious governor and guide.
Now, my guid friends, consider, I beseech,
The cause maist principal of my coming.
No prince or potentate is worth more than a leech,
Who is not guided by my guid governing.
There was never emperor, conqueror nor king
That might without my wisdom mak advance.
My name is Guid Counsel, without feigning,
Lords for lack of my law are brocht to mischance.
Finally, for conclusion,
Who holds me at delusion
Shall be brought to confusion,
And this I understand,
For I have made my residence
With high princes of great puissance,
In England, Italy and France
And mony another land.
But oot of Scotland, whit disgrace!
I have been flingit lang time space,
For them that guide us all want grace
And die before their day.
Because they laughed at Guid Counsel
Fortune turned on them her sail,
Which brocht this realm to falter and fail –
Who can contrairy say?

My Lords, lying is not for me.
Wae's me for King Humanity,
Overset with Sensuality
In his first beginning
Through vicious counsel insolent.
So they may get riches or rent
To his welfare they tak nae tent
Of what shall be the ending.
Yet in this realm I would mak some repair,
If I believed for my name they'd still care.
For, would this King be guided yet with reason,
And punish all wrongdoers with retribution,
Although I have a lang time been away,
I trust in God my name shall yet hold sway.
So, till I see God send mair of His grace,
I purpose to repose me in this place.

Scene 9: The entrance of the Vices

Enter Flattery.

FLATTERY: Make room, sirs, haw! that I may run!
Look, see how I am just come in,
All bedecked in fiery hues –
Let be your din till I begin,
And I shall show you of my news.
Throughout all Christendom I have passed,
And I am come here now at last.
Tossed on the sea since Christmas Day,
That we were fain to hew our mast
Not half a mile beyond the May.
But now amang you I will remain –

I purpose never to sail again,
To put my life at chance in watter.
Never was seen such wind and rain,
Nor of seamen such clitter-clatter!
Some bade 'Hail!' and some bade 'Standby!'
Or 'Starboard, ho!' or 'Port, fie fie!'
While all the ropes began to rattle.
Was never a king as feart as I
When all the sails played brittle-brattle.
To see the waves it was a wonder,
And wind that tore the sails asunder.
But I lay breaking wind as well,
And shat masel, above and under,
The deil would scunner at the smell!
Now I'm escaped from that affray,
What say ye, sirs, am I not gay?
See you not Flattery, your ain fine fool,
That went to mak this new array?
Was I not here with you at Yule?
Aye, by my faith, I think on it weel!
Where are my fellows? Let's dance a reel!
We should be ready for sport at last.
(Falsehood enters.)
Haw! Falsehood, haw!

FALSEHOOD: What the Deil!
Who is it that cries for me so fast?

FLATTERY: Why, Falsehood, brother, d'ye know not me?
Am I not your brother, Flattery?

FALSEHOOD: Now welcome, by the Trinity!
Let me embrace you in my arms.
When friends meet, the heart it warms.

FLATTERY: Where is Deceit, that lowping loon?

FALSEHOOD: I left him drinking in the toon.
              He should be here at ony moment.

FLATTERY: Now, by the Holy Sacrament,
              These tidings comfort all my heart.
              I know Deccit will tak my part.
              He is richt crafty, as ye ken,
              Good counsellor to merchant men.
              Let us baith lie here and spy.
              Maybe we'll see him coming by.

Enter Deceit.

DECEIT: By Christ, what a congregation!
            Are ye all of this one nation?
            Ken ye not, sirs, what is my name?
            Good faith, I dare not show it for shame –
            Though I don't steal, I borrow and len,
            And from my clothing ye may ken
            That I am come of noble men,
            Better you'll never meet.
            I'll argue that with feet and hands!
            I guide the merchants of these lands.
            My name? If ony man demands,
            They call me Deceit.
            Bon jour, brother, with all my heart!
            Here I am come to take your part,
            Into baith guid and evil.
            I met Guid Counsel by the way.
            She nipped my heid, you might weel say.
            I give her to the Devil!
            How came ye here? Pray, do tell me.

FALSEHOOD: To seek out King Humanity.

DECEIT: Since we three seek yon noble King,
Let us devise some subtle thing.
Also I pray you as my brother,
Let us be true to one another.
I mak a vow with all my heart
In good and evil to tak your part.
I pray to God – let me be hanged –
That I shall die before you're wranged.

FALSEHOOD: What is your counsel that we do?

DECEIT: Sirs, this is my counsel true –
Frae time the King begins to stir him,
I dread Guid Counsel will come near him.
Therefore, dear brothers, let's devise
A ploy for going in disguise.

FLATTERY: By God, I'll find a thousand wiles!
We'll turn our coats and change our styles.
We'll mak disguise, that nae man ken us.
(To audience)
Has nae man cleric's cloth to lend us?
(A surplice is thrown to him.)
And let us keep grave countenance,
As though we were just come frae France.

DECEIT: Now, by my soul, that's weel devised!
Soon I too will be disguised.

FALSEHOOD: And so shall I, man, by the Rood.
Now, some good fellow lend me a hood!

Flattery helps the others disguise themselves.

DECEIT: Now I'm dressed up, and who can spy?
              The Devil stick me if this be I!
              If this be I or not I can't well say –
              Or has the Fiend or fairy folk borne me away?

FALSEHOOD: And if my hair were up on my heid,
              The fiend a man would ken me indeed!
              What do ye think of my gay new goun?

DECEIT: I say you look just like a loon!
              Now for you, brother Flattery,
              What kind of man d'ye want to be?

FLATTERY: Now, by my faith, my fellow liar,
              I will go counterfeit a friar.

DECEIT: A friar! But ye cannae preach!

FLATTERY: What matters that? I might well reach,
              By flattering, to highest honour,
              And come to be the King's confessor.

DECEIT: Once I borrowed a friar's hood
              I think on you it would look good.

FLATTERY: Dear friends, it is my heart's desire,
              To go and counterfeit a friar.

DECEIT: Well, this is just the perfect hood
              Aff an auld friar fae Holyrood.

FLATTERY: Who has a prayerbook for to len me?
             Nane but the Fiend himsel will ken me!

FALSEHOOD: If by Correction we be kenned,
             I dreid we'll mak a shameful end.
             We must do more yet, by Saint James –
             We must all three now change our names.
             So christen me, and I'll baptise thee.

DECEIT: By God, and thereabout, may it be!
             What will you call me, I pray thee tell?

FALSEHOOD: I know not what to call mysel!

DECEIT: But you must name the bairn's name.

FALSEHOOD: Discretion! Discretion, in God's name!

DECEIT: Now, sit down, let me baptise thee –
             I know not what your name should be.

FALSEHOOD: But you must name the bairn's name.

DECEIT: Sanity! Sanity, to the world's shame!

FLATTERY: Brother Deceit, come, baptise me.

FALSEHOOD: Then sit down lowly on my knee.

FLATTERY: Now, brother, name the bairn's name.

DECEIT: Devotion! Devotion, in the Devil's name!

FLATTERY: The Devil tak ye, stupid loon!
             You've wet all my new-shaven croon.

DECEIT: Devotion, Sanity and Discretion –
             We three may rule this region.
             We shall find many crafty things
             For to beguile a hundred kings.
             For you can right well crack and clatter,
             And I can feign and you can flatter.

FLATTERY: But I would hae, before we depart,
             A drink to put us in better heart.

DECEIT: Well said, by Him that harried Hell!
             I was just thinking that mysel!

*They drink and watch the King re-enter with Sensuality, the
Courtiers and the Handmaidens.*

Scene 10:   The Vices ingratiate themselves with
the King

KING HUMANITY: Now where is Chill-oot, where is Solace?
                 Where is my minion, Wantonness?
                 Wantonness! Ho! Come to me, son!

WANTONNESS: Come? You called me before I was done!

KING HUMANITY: But what were you doing, tell me, what?

WANTONNESS: Learning how I was begot.
                 Leave Hameliness, my lass, alane.
                 I'd like tae try wi her again.

HAMELINESS: Got ye not what ye desired?
Sir, I believe that ye are tired!

DANGER: As for guid Chill-oot and Solace
I held them baith in merriness.

SOLACE: Now tell me, sir, I you exhort,
Think ye not love a merry sport?

KING HUMANITY: That I do richt verily.
(The Vices approach the King.)
Now who are those men, coming this way?

DECEIT: Laud, honour, glory, triumph, victory
Be to your maist excellent Majesty!

KING HUMANITY: You are welcome, good friends, by the Rood.
You seem to be some men of good.
What are your names? Tell me without delay.

DECEIT: Discretion, sir. That is my name, I'll say.

KING HUMANITY: What's your name, sir, you with the clipped
croon?

FLATTERY: Without a doubt, sir, my name is Devotion.

KING HUMANITY: Welcome, Devotion, of goodly fame.
Now tell me, sir, what is your name?

FALSEHOOD: Well, sir, they call me ... what do they call me?
I know not well, unless I lie!

KING HUMANITY: Can you not tell what is your name?

FALSEHOOD: I kenned it when I came frae hame!

DECEIT: Sanity, you deserve a thick ear!

FALSEHOOD: Sanity! That's it! I know when I hear!

KING HUMANITY: Now why could you not tell me so?

FALSEHOOD: Forgive me, sir, the truth I'll show –
I am so full of Sanity
That sometimes in a trance I'll be.
My spirit rent from my body
Flew high above the Trinity.

KING HUMANITY: Sanity should be a man of good.

FALSEHOOD: Sir, ye may ken that by my hood.

KING HUMANITY: Now I have Sanity and Discretion,
How can I fail to rule this region?
And with Devotion, goodness will flower!
These three came in a happy hour.
(to Deceit)
Here I mak you my secretary,
Of writing noo I'll no be wary.
(to Falsehood)
And you shall be my Treasurer,
(to Flattery)
And you my spiritual counsellor.

FLATTERY: I swear to you, sir, by Saint Ann,
You never met a wiser man.
For mony a craft, sir, do I can,

That you don't know.
I have no feel for flattery,
I'm fostered by philosophy,
A strong man in astronomy,
As I will show.

FALSEHOOD: And I have great intelligence
In questing for the quintessence.
But to prove my experience,
Sir, lend me forty crowns
To mak multiplication.
And tak my obligation,
If we mak false narration,
Hold us to be but clowns!

DECEIT: Sir, I ken by your physiognomy,
You shall conquer, I clearly see,
Gdansk and Germany and land of the Dane,
Castlemilk and castles in Spain.
You shall have at your governance
Renfrew and aw the realm of France,
Rutherglen and the town of Rome,
Corstorphine and all Christendom!
You are, sir, by the Trinity,
The greatest I micht ever see.

FLATTERY: Sir, when I lived in Italy,
I learned the art of palmistry.
Show me the lines, sir, on your hand,
And I shall make you understand
If your Grace be unfortunate,
Or if you be predestinate.
(Looks at the King's hand)

I see ye will have fifteen quines,
And fifteen score of concubines.
The Virgin Mary save your Grace!
Saw ever man so white a face,
So strong an arm, so fair a hand?
There's not such a leg in all this land!
Were you in battle, I'd think it nae wonder
That you would ding doun fifteen hunner!

KING HUMANITY: You are right welcome, by the Rood.
Ye seem to be three men of good.
(He spies Guid Counsel.)
But who is yon that stands so still?
Go and find out what is her will.
And if she yearns for my presence
Bring her to me with diligence.

DECEIT: That shall we do, by God's bread.
We'll bring her, either quick or dead.

FLATTERY: I doubt, my friends, by God himsel,
That yon wumman is Guid Counsel.
If she gets once in the King's presence,
We three will get nae audience.

DECEIT: The matter I shall tak in hand,
And say it is the King's command
That she anon depairt this place
And come not near the guid King's grace,
And that under the pain of treason.

FLATTERY: Brother, I hold your counsel reason.
Now let us hear what she will say.

Scene 11: The Vices repel Guid Counsel

FLATTERY: Guid wumman there, good day, good day!

GUID COUNSEL: Guid day again, sirs, by the Rood.
    May the Lord mak ye men of guid.

DECEIT: Pray not for us to lord or lady,
    For we are men of guid already.
    Now tell us please, what is your name?

GUID COUNSEL: Guid Counsel they call me at hame.

FALSEHOOD: What d'ye say? Are you Guid Counsel?
    Away, ye besom! Go to hell!

GUID COUNSEL: I pray you, sirs, give me licence
    To come into the King's presence,
    To speak but twa words to his Grace.

FLATTERY: False whoor-spawn, now quit this place!

GUID COUNSEL: Brother, I know you well enough
    And why you're making this so tough.
    Flattery, Deceit and False Report,
    That will not suffer to resort
    Guid Counsel to the King's presence.

DECEIT: Be swift, ye whoor-spawn, get ye hence!
    And if you come this way again,
    I swear to God you shall be slain!

GUID COUNSEL: Since at this time the King I canna see,
The remedy is to bide patiently.
Although Guid Counsel hastily be not heard,
Yet with a young prince she should not be scared.
When youthfulness has blown his wanton blast,
Then shall Guid Counsel rule him at the last.

Guid Counsel returns to her place to watch.

Scene 12: The Second Song

KING HUMANITY: What made ye bide so lang from my presence?
I think it lang since you departed thence.
What dame was yon? Why have ye scorned and jeered?
I think she made you, all three, really feared.

FLATTERY: It was a lazy loathsome loon,
Come to housebreak in this toon.
We skelped her lug, though she cried 'Dinnae!'
And sent her packing to Barlinnie.

KING HUMANITY: Let her there repent at leisure,
And let us go and take our pleasure.

SOLACE: Sovereign, before we move along,
Let Sensuality sing us a song.

The Ladies sing a song and the King lounges among them.

ALL FOUR WOMEN: True love is sensual, it's only human –
Love lifts ye up and banishes care.
That spark between a man and a woman –
Nothing else matters, when ye are there.

Love is the reason for every season
And her dance is nature's way.
As every lover comes to discover
Love brightens every day.

True love's essential, it's only human.
Love lifts ye up and banishes care.
That fire between a man and a woman.
Everything matters when ye are there.

Love is the reason for every season
And her dance maks a' thing richt.
As every lover comes to discover
Love sweetens every nicht.

Scene 13: The entrance of Verity

Enter Verity; carrying a book.

VERITY: Diligite Justitiam qui judicatis terram.
            Ye judges of the earth, set your affection on wisdom.
            Kings should of guid example be the well,
            But if those waters be a toxic spring,
            Instead of wine, they drink the poison fell –
            The fickle people follow aye their King.
            (Flattery sees Verity and stares at her; dumbstruck.)
            If men of me would have intelligence
            Or know my name, they call me Verity.
            Of the Lord's law I have experience
            And have sailed over many a stormy sea.
            Now I am seeking King Humanity,
            I have the greatest hopes for his good grace.

When he becomes acquainted well with me,
Honour and Glory he will soon embrace.

DECEIT: Guid day, faither, where have ye been?
What news is there, I pray ye tell?

FLATTERY: I have this very moment seen
Dame Verity, by book and bell!
But come she to the King's presence,
There is no way for us to bide,
Therefore I say we should go hence.

DECEIT: That will we not, by good Saint Bride;
But we shall either go or ride
To Lords of Spirituality.
Get them to say yon bag of pride
Has spoken manifest heresy.

They address the Spiritual Estaite.

FLATTERY: O reverent fathers of the spiritual state,
We counsel you be wise and vigilant
Dame Verity has lighted here of late,
In her hand bearing the New Testament.
Be she received, we three must be absent.
Let her not lodge therefore in this country –
We bid you do it now, let her be sent,
While the King wi his love sleeps sae peacefully.

BISHOP: We thank you, friends, for your benevolence.
It shall be done, even as you have devised.
And you deserve a goodly recompense,
Defending us that we be not surprised.

PRIORESS: I hold it best for safety's sake that we
Should hold her fast into captivity,
And then accuse her of her heresy
And banish her from out of this country.

BISHOP: Now, Parson, you shall be my emissary
To put this matter into execution.
And if she speaks against our liberty,
Then put her in perpetual prison.

The Parson and the three Vices approach Verity.

PARSON: Lusty Lady, we would fain understand
What errand ye have here in this region.
To preach or teach, who gave to you command?
To counsel kings, how got you this commission?
I dreid, unless you are granted some remission
And gie up new ideas that mak us moan,
The Spiritual Estaite shall damn you to perdition,
And in the fire will burn you, flesh and bone.

VERITY: I will recant naething that I have shown.
I have said naething but the verity.
As for the King, when I to him am known,
All you that spout of spirituality
Shall rue the day I came into this country,
For if the verity plainly be proclaimed,
And specially to the King's Majesty,
For your traditions you will all be defamed.

FLATTERY: What book is that, harlot, held in your hand?
Out! Get away! This is the New Testament,
In English tongue and printed in England!
Heresy! Heresy! Fire be your punishment!

VERITY: Forsooth, my friend, you have a wrang judgement,
           For in this book there is nae heresy,
           But our Christ's word, baith sweet and redolent,
           A springing well of sincere verity.

DECEIT: Come on your way, for all your yellow locks!
           Your wanton words, doubt not, ye shall repent.
           This nicht ye'll suffer here, clamped in the stocks,
           And in the morn be brocht to thole judgement.

VERITY: For our Christ's sake, I am richt weel content
           To suffer all things that shall please His grace.
           Although you put a thousand to torment,
           Ten hundred thousand shall rise and take their place.
           Now, Lords, do of yir best –
           I have nae mair to say.

FLATTERY: Sit doon and tak yir rest
           All nicht till it be day!

They put her in the stocks and return to Spirituality.

DECEIT: My Lord, we have with diligence
           Buckled up well yon blethering bard.

BISHOP: Then you deserve good recompense,
           Take here ten crowns for your reward.

Scene 14: The entrance of Chastity

Enter Chastity.

CHASTITY: How long shall this inconstant world endure,
That I should banished be so long, alas?
To care for me there is not one creature,
And mony a nicht I'm hameless, by the Mass.
Though I have passed all year from place to place,
Amang the Temporal and Spiritual estates,
Yet amang princes I can get nae grace –
They haud me back richt roughly at their gates.

DILIGENCE: Lady, I pray you, tell to me your name,
It vexes me, this moaning, sae pipe doon!

CHASTITY: My friend, thereof I need not speak wi shame –
Dame Chastity, banished frae toon tae toon.

DILIGENCE: But here are holy women, dinna frown –
They mak their vows to observe chastity.
Look, there sits a prioress of renown
Amang the rest of Spirituality.

CHASTITY: I grant yon lady has vowed chastity,
For her profession thereto should accord.
She made that vow so she'd be sitting pretty,
But not for Christ Jesus our Lord.
They mak their vows, the Spirituality,
But banish Chastity oot o their company
Whiles I maun walk a road that's hard and gritty,
They lead their lives in sensuality.

(To Prioress)

My prudent, lusty Lady Prioress,
Remember how you did vow Chastity.
Madame, I pray you of your gentleness
Do give me shelter. Prove your sanctity.

PRIORESS: Pass hence, Madame, by Christ you mak us tire!
You're contrary to my complexion.
Go seek a room wi some auld monk or friar
Perchance they may be your protection.
Or unto prelates mak now your progression,
Who are obliged to you as well as I.
Dame Sensual has given me direction
That you my company I should deny.

CHASTITY: Lords, in this land I can get no lodging.
If you should want my name to be knowing,
Forsooth, my Lords, they call me Chastity.
Give me lodging this night, for charity!

BISHOP: Pass on, Madame, tae us you're nought,
Or by Him that the world has wrought,
Your coming shall be richt dear bought
If you should longer tarry.
Doubt not that we will live and die
With our love, Sensuality.
And we will nae mair deal with thee
Than with the Queen of Fairy!

PARSON: Pass hame amang the nuns and dwell,
Who are of chastity the well –
I trust they will with book and bell
Receive you in their cloister.

CHASTITY: When with the nuns I did reside,
             They drove me out, by good Saint Bride,
             And let me not so long there bide
             To say my Pater Noster.
             If I try there, lang time I'll wait –
             I hold it best before it's late
             To try the Temporal Estaite,
             If they will me receive.
             (To Temporality and Merchant)
             Good day, my Lord Temporality,
             And you, Merchant of gravity,
             I beg that you will suffer me
             To lodge here, by your leave.

MERCHANT: Forsooth, we would be weel content
             To harbour you with guid intent
             If we had not impediment –
             For why? We are baith married!

TEMPORALITY: And if my wife knew you were here,
             She'd mak the hail toon turn gey queer.
             Therefore you should retreat for fear
             She harm you – I'd be worried.

CHASTITY: Ye men of craft, of skill maist fine,
             Give me shelter, by Christ, I pine –
             And win God's blessing, aye, and mine,
             And help my hungry heart!

Soutar and Taylor come forward from the Temporal Estaite. They are observed by Taylor's daughter, Jenny.

SOUTAR: Welcome, by Him that made the moon,
          To dwell with us till it be June.
          Come ower here and sit ye doon.
          We'll plainly tak yer part.

TAYLOR: Is this fair Lady Chastity?
          Now welcome, by the Trinity!
          I think it is a great pity
          That you should be pit oot –

SOUTAR: It isnae right, that's what I think.
          Sit doon, Madame, and tak a drink,
          And don't let sorrow in you sink.
          (*He brings out a hip-flask, offers it.*)
          Huv a swally, turn aboot!

They sit down and drink.

JENNY: Haw there, Mammy! Mammy! Mammy!

Enter Mrs Taylor and Mrs Soutar.

MRS TAYLOR: Whit is it, lassie? Whit's the rammy?
              Jenny, my darling, where's yer daddy?

JENNY: He's drinking wi a lusty lady,
         A fair young maiden dressed in white.
         In her my daddy takes delight.
         I trust if I can reckon right,
         She plans to lodge wi him all night.

MRS SOUTAR: Where is that Soutar, my good man?

JENNY: He fills the cup and tips the can –
                         I think he disnae give a fig,
                         He will be drunker than a pig.

MRS TAYLOR: What a disgrace to find out how
                         They sit there drinking wi this cow.
                         What do ye think? What shall we do?

MRS SOUTAR: Here's my advice, I've thought it through –
                         You clout the one, and I the other!

MRS TAYLOR: I like that fine, by God's guid mother!
                         I'm telling you, they whooring scum
                         Deserve a skelp across the bum.
                         What fiend accounts for all this haste?
                         For it is half a year, almaist,
                         Since that loon climbed aboard his wife.

MRS SOUTAR: The same wi mine, for by my life,
                         I swear it's mair than forty days
                         Since ever he cleiked up my claes.
                         And last time we started to screw,
                         That foul Soutar began to spew.

MRS TAYLOR: And now they will sit down and drink,
                         Wi this foul whoor, this tousie tink!

MRS SOUTAR: They're doing this their wives to spite.
                         We'll go and shake them till they shite!

The wives chase away Chastity.

MRS TAYLOR: Go hence, harlot! How dare ye be so bold
To lodge wi our goodmen in our absence?
I mak a vow to Him that Judas sold,
This rock of mine shall be your recompense.
Tell me your name, you slut, with diligence!

CHASTITY: My name is Chastity, by guid Saint Blaise.

MRS SOUTAR: I pray that God may wreak on you vengeance,
For never I loved Chastity all my days!

MRS TAYLOR: I vow if you come by this way again,
Your buttocks shall be belted, by Saint Blaine!

The wives turn to their husbands.

MRS SOUTAR: False whoor-son dog, you will regret it now,
That ever you sat drinking wi yon cow!

MRS TAYLOR: I mak a vow to Saint Crispin,
I'll wipe your face of that graceless grin,
And to begin the play, tak that! And that!

TAYLOR: The Fiend receive the hands that gave me that!

MRS TAYLOR: What now, whoor-son? Your protest is too late.
Tak there another on your baldy pate!
(To Mrs Soutar)
Come now, sister, will you not take my part?

MRS SOUTAR: That I will do, sister, with all my heart!
(The wives chase their husbands off.)

Scene 15: Chastity approaches the King

DILGENCE: *(To Chastity)*
              Madame, why do you walk so late?
              Tell me how you have made debate
              With Temporal and Spiritual Estaite.
              Who showed you most kindness?

CHASTITY: In faith, it went from bad to worse –
              They drove me from them with a curse,
              Like some puir beggar wi nae purse,
              Disowned me mair or less.

They go towards the King and his courtiers.

DILIGENCE: Ho! Solace, gentle Solace, declare unto the King
              How there is here a lady, fair of face,
              That in this country can get nae lodging –
              She's pitifully driven from place to place,
              Unless the King by his almighty grace
              Receive her as a servant in his court
              Brother Solace, put to him the case,
              For this is now a matter of some import.

SOLACE: *(to King)*
              Sovereign, get up and see a heavenly sight,
              A fair lady all dressed in purest white.
              She may be peer unto a king or knight,
              Most like an angel, radiant and bright.

KING HUMANITY: I shall go see that sight without delay.
              (to Sensuality)
              Madame, tell me if you know anything

About that lady fair who comes this way.
Then I shall see her without tarrying.

SENSUALITY: Sir, let me see who yon lady may be –
Perchance that I may know her by her face.
But, without doubt, this is Dame Chastity!
Sir, I and she cannot bide in one place.
But if it be the pleasure of your grace
That I remain here in your company,
Then this woman richt hastily go chase,
Oot o this country and far across the sea.

KING HUMANITY: Whatever you please, sweetheart, so declare I.
Dispose of her some way expedient.
Even as you wish, to let her live or die,
I will refer it to your good judgement.

SENSUALITY: I will that from this place she should be sent,
Never again in this country to lie.
And if she does, but doubt she shall repent,
And then perchance a doleful death she'll die.
Pass on, Sir Sanity and Sir Discretion,
And banish her out of the King's presence.

FLATTERY: That shall we do, Madame, by the guid Lord's
passion.
We shall do your command with diligence.
(To Chastity)
Dame Chastity, come on, be not aghast.
Into the stocks your bonny foot mak fast!

CHASTITY: Sister, alas, this surely is a crime,
That we by princes should be so abhorred.

VERITY: Be blyth, sister, within short space of time
We shall baith be richt honourably restored,
And with the King we shall be at concord.
For I hear whispered furth Divine Correction
Is newly landed, thanked be Christ our Lord.
I know to all guid folk he'll give protection.

Scene 16: The entrance of Correction's Varlet

Enter Divine Correction's Varlet.

VARLET: Sirs, stand ye back, give me the stage!
I am the King Correction's page
Come to prepare his place.
See that ye mak obedience
Unto his noble excellence
When you look on his face.
For he maks reformations
Throughout all Christian nations
Where he finds great debates.
And so far as I understand,
He shall reform throughout this land
Even all the Three Estaites.
God furth of Heaven him did send
To punish all that do offend
Against His Majesty.
As he likes best to tak vengeance
Sometimes wi sword and pestilence
Wi dearth and poverty.
But when the people do repent
And are to God obedient
Then will he give them grace.

But they that will not be corrected,
Richt suddenly will be ejected
And banished from his face.

Scene 17: The Vices flee

DECEIT: Brother, hear ye thon proclamation?
I dreid full sair this reformation.
That message has me stung.
What's your advice? To me now tell.
If we bide here, by God Himsel,
We three will all be hung!

FLATTERY: I'll gang to Spirituality,
And preach in some locality
Where I will be unknown.
Or keep me close into some cloister
Wi many a pious Pater Noster,
Till all their blasts be blown.

DECEIT: I'll be well treated, as ye ken,
By my maisters, the merchant men
Who need, sometimes, to cheat.
Ye ken right few of them that thrives
Or can beguile their country wives
Without their friend Deceit.
Now, Falsehood, how quit ye this mess?

FALSEHOOD: Naw, care ye nocht for my success –
Think you that I be daft?
Now I will live a lusty life,
Without fear of trouble or strife
Among the men of craft.

FLATTERY: I no more will remain beside you.

                  I pray the Fairy Queen will guide you.

Flattery goes to sit among the Spiritual Estaite.

DECEIT: *(to Falsehood)*

          Falsehood, friend, our bond let's keep,

          And while the King is still asleep,

          Now we can steal his box.

FALSEHOOD: Now, well said, by the Sacrament!

          To crack it open's my intent,

          Though it had twenty locks!

          (He steals the King's treasure chest.)

          Here's the box! Now let us gae!

          This may suffice for our rewards.

DECEIT: Aye, that it may, and by this day,

          It may well mak us landed lords.

          Now let us cast away these claes,

          For fear some follow and give chase.

FALSEHOOD: Richt weel devised, man, by Saint Blaise.

          Would God we were out of this place!

They throw away their disguises.

DECEIT: Now, since there is nae man tae wrang us,

          I pray you, brother, with my heart,

          Let us go split the spoils between us,

          Since hastily we shall depart.

FALSEHOOD: You think to get as much as I?
That shall you not! I stole the box!
You did nothing but look by,
Aye lurking like a wily fox!

DECEIT: Your heid shall bear a couple of knocks –
Richt, pal – unless I get my part!
Sod off, ya bastard, smash open the locks,
Or else I'll stick you through the heart!

They fight.

FALSEHOOD: Oh my God! My eye is out!

DECEIT: Too bad, now tak another clout!

*Deceit runs away with the box to the Merchants. Falsehood
staggers off to sit amongst Temporality.*

Scene 18: The entrance of Divine Correction

Divine Correction appears above with a drawn sword.

CORRECTION: If ony need my name for to enquire,
Hear ye now, I am called Divine Correction.
I've cut through mony an uncouth land and shire
To bring each nation closer to perfection.
Nae realm withoot support of me may stand,
For I mak kings face up to royalty.
To rich and poor I show an equal hand
That they may flourish to their due degree.

Where I am nocht is nae tranquillity.
By me traitors and tyrants are put doon
Who think no shame of their iniquity
Till they be punished by me, Divine Correction.
I will do nocht without there first being called
A Parliament of the Estaites all.
Into their presence tyrants shall be hauled.
Under my sword iniquity shall fall.
What is a king? Nocht but an officer
To cause his liegcs live in equity,
And under God to be the punisher
Of trespassers against His majesty.
But if a king's true subjects live in fear
Then justice demands the king be brocht tae trial.
I am a judge, richt potent and severe,
Come to do justice mony a thousand mile.
There is, therefore, richt mony in this isle
Of my arrival no doubt will repent.
But virtuous men, I trust, shall on me smile,
And of my coming be richt weel content.

GUID COUNSEL: Welcome, my Lord, welcome ten thousand times
From faithful folk that dwell here in this region!
Welcome for to correct all faults and crimes
Among this crabbit cankered congregation!
Loose Chastity, I mak you supplication,
Put to freedom fair Lady Verity,
Who by the unfaithful folk of this nation
Lies bound full fast here in captivity.

CORRECTION: I marvel, Guid Counsel, how that may be.
Do ye not with the King disport?

GUID COUNSEL: That I do not, my Lord, full woe is me!
But like a beggar I dwell outside the court.
For, skulking in under an evil star,
There came three knaves in clothing counterfeit,
And from the King they made me stand afar.
Their names are Flattery, Falsehood and Deceit.
They hid in the Estaites when you cam near
With Merchants, Craftsmen and Spirituality.

CORRECTION: Doubt not, my friend, before I gang from here,
I shall search out that great iniquity.
Go put yon ladies to their liberty
Straight away, and break down all the stocks!
Doubt not they are full dear welcome to me.
Speed hand and spare not for to break the locks,
And tenderly tak them up by the hand.
Had I them here, they knaves should ken my knocks,
That them oppressed and banished off the land!

Chastity and Verity are freed from the stocks.

CHASTITY: We thank you, Sir, for your benignity,
But I beseech your Majesty royal
That you would go to King Humanity
And free him from yon Lady Sensual.

CORRECTION: Come then, sisters, I'll do as I am able,
And mak him stand with you three, firm and stable.

He moves towards the King with Verity, Chastity and Guid Counsel.

Scene 19: Divine Correction comes to the King

WANTONNESS: Solace, know you not what I see?
A knight or a king it seems to me.
Wi blazing blade and fiery ee.
What think you this might mean?
I cannot say, I do not know
Whether he be friend or foe.
I'm sure he's brocht a tale of woe
The like I've never seen!

SOLACE: He is a stranger, by my accord.
He seems to be a lusty lord.
If he comes here to make concord
And be kind to our King,
He shall be welcome to this place,
And treated with the King's guid grace.
Be that not so, we shall him chase,
And to the Devil him ding!

CHILL-OOT: I counsel we approach the King,
And waken him from his sleeping.
Sir, rise and see an uncouth thing!
Get up, ye lie too lang!

SENSUALITY: Now haud yer wheesht and dinna rave!
How dare ye be so pert, Sir Knave,
To touch the King? So Christ me save,
False whoor-son, you shalt hang!

CORRECTION: Get up, Sir King! For ye have slept enough
               Wrapped in the arms of Sensuality!
               A sovereign should be made of stronger stuff
               And not be caught by damsels of such quality.
               Remember how, before the time of Troy
               For the foul stink and sin of lechery
               God by my sword did all the world destroy.
               Sodom and Gomorrah richt rigorously
               For that vile sin were burnt most cruelly.
               Therefore I do command you, Sir, tak tent!
               Banish from you that whoor Sensuality,
               Or else but doubt you rudely shall repent!

KING HUMANITY: By whom have ye such great authority
               Who does presume for to correct a king?
               Know ye not me, great King Humanity,
               That in this region wears the royal ring?

CORRECTION: My power the greatest princes down can bring,
               That live opposed to Majesty Divine.
               And for the truth, they know not such a thing –
               Repent they not, I'll mak them toe the line.
               I will begin with you, who is the head,
               And mak on you first reformation.
               Your lieges then will follow where they're led.
               (To Sensuality)
               But you, whoor! Hence without hesitation!

SENSUALITY: Adieu, Sir King, I can no longer tarry.
               But I care not – as good life comes as goes.
               I recommend you to the Queen of Fairy –
               I see you will be guided by my foes.

(To the Bishop)
My Lord, although this parting does me pain,
I trust in God we shall meet soon again.

BISHOP: Sweet lady fair, that is my heart's desire.
Withoot ye here, my life will lack all fire.

Sensuality and her ladies exit while exchanging lingering kisses with the Spiritual Estaite.

Scene 20: The End of Part One

CORRECTION: *(To King)*
Now you are quit of Sensuality,
Receive into your service Guid Counsel,
And richt so this fair Lady Chastity,
Till you marry some queen of blood royal –
Observe then chastity matrimonial.
Receive here also Verity by the hand –
Use their counsel, your fame will never fall.
With them, therefore, make a perpetual band.
(The King receives Guid Counsel, Chastity and Verity.)
Now sir, tak tent what I will say –
Observe the same baith night and day,
Let them not be from you away,
Or else, without a doubt,
Turn ye to Sensuality,
To vicious life and ribaldry,
Out of your realm richt shamefully
You shall be rooted out!

KING HUMANITY: I am content your counsel to incline.
                  At your command shall be all that is mine.
                  And here I give unto you full commission
                  To punish faults or else to grant remission.

The King embraces Divine Correction, with a humble countenance.

CORRECTION: I counsel you, as God me sent,
               To go proclaim a Parliament
               Of all the Thrie Estaites,
               That they be here with diligence
               To mak to you obedience
               And address all debates.

KING HUMANITY: That shall be done, as you command.
                  Ho, Diligence! Come here to hand,
                  And tak your information.
                  Go warn the Spirituality,
                  Merchants and Temporality,
                  By open proclamation,
                  In goodly haste for to appear,
                  Maist honourably to come here
                  To give us their advice.
                  Who dare be absent, show therefore,
                  That they shall stand the law before,
                  And punished for that vice.

DILIGENCE: Sir, I shall in burgh and land
              With diligence do your command
              Upon my own expense.
              Sir, I have done your bidding sweet,
              And never got a bite to eat
              To be my recompense.

KING HUMANITY: Go, and you'll be weel regarded,
And for your service weel rewarded!
For look, with my consent,
You shall have yearly for your hire,
The oyster-beds of Lanarkshire,
Confirmed in Parliament.

DILIGENCE: I will get riches through that rent
After the Day of Doom,
When in the coalpits of Tranent,
Butter will grow on broom!
All nicht I had a meikle drouth,
I never slept a wink.
Before I proclaim with my mooth,
I'll need to hae a drink.

CORRECTION: Come here now, Chill-oot and Solace
With your companion Wantonness.
You must be penitent.
For tempting King Humanity
To receive Sensuality
You'll suffer punishment.

WANTONNESS: We grant, my Lord, we have done ill,
Therefore we bow before thy will,
But we have been abused.
For in good faith, sir, we believed
That lechery had no man grieved
Because it is so used.

CHILL-OOT: You see how Sensuality
With principals of each country
Was gladly allowed in.

And with our prelates, none the less –
Go ask my Lady Prioress
If lechery be sin!

SOLACE: Sir, we shall mend our condition,
If you grant to us remission,
But give us leave to sing,
To dance, to play at chess and tables,
To read ripe tales and merry fables
For pleasure of our King.

CORRECTION: So that ye do no other crime,
You shall be pardoned at this time.
This thought now I give voice –
Princes may sometimes seek solace
With mirth and lawful merriness,
Their spirits to rejoice.

KING HUMANITY: Where is Sanity? Where's Discretion?
And comes not my friend Devotion?

VERITY: The truth, sir, if I would report –
They did beguile your Excellence,
And would not suffer to resort
One of us three to your presence.

CHASTITY: They three were Flattery and Deceit,
And Falsehood, that unhappy loon.
Against us they did lies repeat
And banished us fae toon tae toon.
They made us two fall in a swoon
When they did lock us in the stocks.
That dastard knave, Discretion,
The sneaky thief did steal your box.

KING HUMANITY: The Devil tak them, now they're fled,
But if I catch them, they'll be dead!
Good Counsel, now show me the best,
How I shall keep my realm at rest.

GOOD COUNSEL: Sire, you are but mortal instrument
To that great God and King omnipotent.
The principal point of any guid King's span
Is to do justice for each and every man,
And to mix his justice with clemency,
Without rigour, favour or partiality.
Whoever takes on him the role of King
Is sure to get one or the other thing –
Great pain and labour, and that continual,
Or suffer defamation perpetual.
Who guides well wins immortal fame,
If the contrair, they get perpetual shame.
For every prince that justice holds on high,
Though he be dead, his deeds shall never die.
If you desire to rule this country well,
I bid thee, Sir, attend to Guid Counsel.

DILIGENCE: Oyez! Oyez! Oyez!
At the command of King Humanity,
I warn and charge all members of Parliament,
Baith Spiritual State and Temporality,
That to his grace you be obedient,
To come here to the court is maist expedient.
His royal order you must all obey.
Whoever's absent or disobedient
The King's displeasure they shall feel this day.

(To bulk of audience)
And now I do exhort you, leave your seat,
Since you have heard the first part of our play,
Go tak a drink and get a bite to eat –
Tarry not long, it is late in the day.
And if ye need tae have a slash,
Intae the bogs now ye must dash
Tae let it rip and mak a splash.
Dae what ye have tae dae!
Let not your bladder burst, I pray you,
For that would be enough to slay you!
For yet there is to come, I pray you,
The best part of our play!

(INTERVAL)

The 3 Estaites

Part Two

Scene 21: The entrance of the Poor Man

The audience returns and Part Two begins. The King, Bishop and principal players are not yet in their seats. Fanfare. Diligence begins a proclamation.

DILIGENCE: Famous people, tak tent and ye shall see
The Thrie Estaites of this nation...

Enter a Poor Man, interrupting; addressing members of the audience.

POOR MAN: Big Issue! Big Issue! Jist oot the day!
Big Issue! Big Issue! What's that ye say?
You've already got it? Is that what he said?
Buy another ya bastard! It's only a quid!

DILIGENCE: In the name o God! Somebody hose him doon!
Get yourself oot o here, false whoorson ragged
loon!

POOR MAN: Gie me alms, guid folks, for God's love of Heaven,
For I have motherless bairns, six or seven.
If you'll gie me nae guid, for Jesus' sake,
The road to Glasgow I'll have to take.

DILIGENCE: I thought this was a safe and well-kept place.
For beggars like this to get in, it's a disgrace!
Unless ye come and chase this churl away,
The devil a word you'll get more of this play!
(The Poor Man climbs up to the King's throne.)
Come doon, or by God's croon, false loon, I'll slay ye!

POOR MAN: Threaten all that ye want. The Devil flay ye!

DILIGENCE: Loup doon, or by the Guid Lord, ye shall lose yer heid!

POOR MAN: I'll tak a drink to that, though you had sworn me deid!

He swigs the King's drink and leaps down.

DILIGENCE: Hence, beggar bogle, haste ye away!
You're ower pert to spoil our play!

POOR MAN: I wouldnae gie for your auld play a sow's fart,
For there's richt little play in my hungry heart!

DILIGENCE: What devil ails this crooked churl?

POOR MAN: Marry, meikle sorrow.
I cannae get, though I gasp, to beg or to borrow.

DILIGENCE: Where, devil, do you dwell? And what's your intent?

POOR MAN: I live in Lothian, a mile frae Tranent.

DILIGENCE: Where are you going? Tell me it true.

POOR MAN: To seek the law. What is it to you?

DILIGENCE: To seek law in Edinburgh's the easiest way.

POOR MAN: Sir, I sought it there mony a dear day,
But at Session or Synod naething I got,
Therefore the Devil drown the whole lot!

DILIGENCE: Tell me your trouble, with all the circumstances,
How you have happened on these unhappy chances

POOR MAN: Guid man, will you give me your charity,
And I shall declare to you the black verity.
My father was an auld man, wi grey hair,
His age it was fourscore of years and mair.
And Maud my mother lived ninety years in pain,
And with my labour I did them baith sustain.
We had one mare that carried salt and coal,
And every year she brought us hame a foal.
We had three cows that were baith fat and fair,
Nane tidier in all the toon of Ayr.
My faither was so weak of blood and bone,
That he died, and so my mother made great moan.
Then she died, within a day or so,
And there began my poverty and woe.
Our guid grey mare was grazin – here's the facts –
When our landlord took her for council tax.
The Bishop took the best cow by the heid,
Quick as ye like when my faither was deid.
And when the Bishop heard tell that my mother
Was deid as well, he took from me another.
Then Meg my wife did mourn evening and morrow,
Till at the last she died for very sorrow.
And when the Bishop heard my wife was deid,
The third cow he cleikit by the heid.
Even their hamespun claes sae coarse and grey,
The Bishop's clarty clerk bore them away.
When all was gone, I want this understood,
Wi my poor bairns I had to beg for food.
Now I have told ye the black verity,
How I am brought into this misery.
In good faith, Sir, though ye would cut my throat,
Nae mair than these few pennies have I got –
All I can pay to hire a man of law.

DILIGENCE: You are the daftest fool that ever I saw!
D'ye think, man, that the law for you will plead
Against the kirk? No! Not till you be deid!
Be sure from priests you will get nae support.

POOR MAN: If that be true, the Fiend receive the sort!
And since I see I'll get no other grace,
I will lie doon and rest me in this place.

He lies down to sleep. Enter Flattery, in his disguise as a friar.

Scene 22: The Pardoner and the Soutars

FLATTERY: Bona dies, Bona dies!
Devout people, Good day I say to you.
Now tarry a little while, I pray to you,
Till I be with you known.
Ken ye no weel how I am named?
A noble man and undefamed
If aa the truth were shown.
I am Sir Robert Roll-Over,
A perfect, public pardoner,
And sanctioned by the Pope.
Sirs, I shall show ye for my wage
My pardons and my privilege,
And I shall sell ye hope.
My patent pardons aye sae holy
I got frae yon great Ayatollie.
Weel sealed wi oyster shells.
Though ye have nae contrition,
Ye shall have full remission
Wi help o books and bells.

Here is a cord – the truth I tell –
That hanged yon Peter Manuel,
Of guid hemp soft and sound.
Guid halie people – I'm nae dope –
Whoever be hanged wi this here rope
Needs never tae be drowned!
Who loves their wife nocht wi their heart,
I have the power them to part –
I think you're deaf and dumb!
Has nane of you cursed wicked wife
That hauds ye doon and gies ye strife?
Attend tae me now, come!

SOUTAR: *(Coming out of the crowd)*
Welcome hame, Robert Roll-Over,
Our halie patent pardoner!
If ye have dispensation
To part me and my wicked wife,
Deliver me frae trouble and strife,
I mak you supplication.

FLATTERY: I shall ye part as ye demand
When I get some cash in my hand.
Therefore, let's see yer money!

SOUTAR: I've nae cash on me but, by my life,
I've credit in every bank in Fife.
(Shows credit cards.)
Take one, I'm no being funny.

FLATTERY: What kind of wumman is yer wife?

SOUTAR: A quick devil, Sir, a storm of strife,
           A fiend that fouls the air,
           A fetid fart, a flichty tart,
           A fearsome fricht, she breaks my heart
           And brings me tae despair.
           Aa the lang day she spits oot spite
           And aa the nicht she'll fling and flyte,
           So I sleep never a wink.
           That cockteaser, that common whoor –
           The Devil himself could nocht endure
           Her stubbornness and stink!

MRS SOUTAR: *(Coming out of the crowd)*
             Thief! Churl! Yer words I heard richt weel!
             In faith, my friendship ye shall feel
             Before too lang!

SOUTAR: If I said ocht, Dame, by the Rood,
           Except that ye were fair and guid,
           God let me hang!

FLATTERY: Fair dame, if ye would gang awa,
           I have the power tae part ye twa.
           Tell on, are ye content?

MRS SOUTAR: Aye, that I am with all my heart,
             Frae that false whoor-son I'll depart
             If this thief will consent.
             A cause to part? I'll no be coy –
             In bed he cannae gie me joy,
             I tell ye, it's nae lie.
             But it's nae wonder, I'm telling you,
             Yon useless bastard cannae screw –
             He is baith cauld and dry.

FLATTERY: What will ye gie me, for your part?

MRS SOUTAR: *(Shows credit card.)*
              My guid gowd kerd, wi all my heart,
              The finest in the land.

FLATTERY: To part, then, ye are baith content,
              As soon as it's convenient,
              But first, here's my command.
              My will and final sentence is –
              Each one the other's arse must kiss!
              Slip doon yer hose. She isnae gonnae poke it!
              Turn not away, although she kiss and soak it!
              (Mrs Soutar kisses Soutar's arse in silence.)
              Lift up her claes! Kiss her hole wi all your heart!

SOUTAR: I pray ye, Sir, forbid her for to fart!

(Soutar kisses his wife's arse in silence.)

FLATTERY: Dame, pass ye tae the east end o the toon,
              And pass ye west even like a cuckold loon.
              Go hence, ye baith, wi the Deil's ain blessing!
              (The Soutars exit.)
              Did ever ye see a mair sorrowless parting?

Scene 23: The Pardoner and the Poor Man

POOR MAN: *(Sitting up)*
              What thing was yon I heard? My mind I'll lose!
              I have been dreaming and gibbering of my coos.
              I see standing yonder a haily man.

To gie me help, let me see if he can.
Haily maister, God speed you and good morn!

FLATTERY: Welcome to you! Although your face is torn!
Come, win my pardon, and then I'll bless you, sir.

POOR MAN: Will that pardon get me my coos once mair?

FLATTERY: Sir, wi your coos I have nothing to dae.
Come, win my pardon, and kiss my relics tae!
Now, loose your purse good man, or you are lost.

POOR MAN: My haily faither, what will the pardon cost?

FLATTERY: Let me see what cash you carry in your bag.

POOR MAN: I hae a few pence wrapped up in a rag.

FLATTERY: Are these few pennies all that you have got?

POOR MAN: If I hae mair, sir, come and rip my coat!

FLATTERY: Give me your pennies, if ye have nae mair.

POOR MAN: With all my heart, maister, take it, there!
Now let me see your pardon, as I live.

FLATTERY: A thousand years of pardons here I give.

POOR MAN: A thousand year? I will not live so lang!
Deliver it tae me, and let me gang.

FLATTERY: You have received your pardon now already.

POOR MAN: But I can see naething, sir, by Our Lady!

FLATTERY: What crave you, churl? I think you are not wise!

POOR MAN: I'll hae my pennies or the merchandise!

FLATTERY: I gave you pardon for a thousand year.

POOR MAN: How shall I get that pardon? Let me hear.

FLATTERY: Stand still and I shall tell you the hail story –
When you are deid and go to Purgatory,
You'll be condemned to pain a thousand year.
Then shall the pardon save you, have no fear.
Now be content, maist marvellous of men!

POOR MAN: Shall I get nothing for my cash till then?

FLATTERY: That you shall not. I tell it to you plain.

POOR MAN: Naw? Right, big mooth, gie me my cash again!

FLATTERY: Away! Stand back! You stinking heap of dung!
You'll not get this back, though you should be hung!

POOR MAN: Give me my pennies, wrapped up in their cloot,
Or by Christ, sir, I'll knock all your teeth oot!

They fight. The Poor Man knocks over Flattery's pardoning table and throws the relics away.

Scene 24: The Thrie Estaites gang backward

DILIGENCE: What kind of carry-on is this all day?
              Daft gowks, get out of here, away!

*The Poor Man chases Flattery offstage. Diligence launches into his
proclamation.*

              Famous people, tak tent and ye shall see
              The Thrie Estaites of this nation
              Come to the court with a strange gravity.
              Therefore I mak you supplication
              Till ye have heard our hail narration
              To keep silence and be patient I pray you.
              Although we shall give explanation,
              We shall say nothing but the truth, I tell you.

*As the King, Divine Correction, the Courtiers, the Virtues and the
Sergeants come on, the representatives of the Thrie Estaites enter
backwards, led by their Vices.*

WANTONNESS: By the Lord God almighty!
              What thing is yon that I see?
              Look, Solace, be on guard!

SOLACE: Brother Wantonness, what think you?
              Yon are the Thrie Estaites, it's true,
              Gangin backward!

WANTONNESS: So let us go and tell the King.
              (They turn to the King.)
              Sir, we have seen a marvellous thing
              By our judgement.

SOLACE: The Thrie Estaites of this region
Are coming backwards through the toon
To the Parliament!

KING HUMANITY: Backward? Backward? How may that be?
Go speed them hastily to me
For fear that they go wrang.

CHILL-OOT: Sir, I see them yonder coming –
They're making moan, chanting and humming –
As fast as they can gang.

GUID COUNSEL: Sir, hold you still and scare them not
Till you perceive what be their thought
And what brought them to this.
Then let the King Correction
Mak a sharp inquisition
To find out what's amiss.
When ye ken the occasion
That makes for this persuasion
Ye may deal wi the cause,
Then them reform as ye think best,
So that the realm may live in rest
According to God's laws.

BISHOP: Glory, honour, laud, triumph, victory
Be to your michty, prudent Excellence!
Here are we come, all the Estaites Thrie,
Ready to mak our due obedience
At your command, with humble observance,
As may pertain to Spirituality
With counsel of the Temporality.

TEMPORALITY: Sir, we with mighty courage at command
                 Of your superexcellent Majesty
                 Shall mak service baith with our heart and hand,
                 And shall not dread in your defence to die.
                 We are content, doubt not, that we may see
                 That noble heavenly King Correction
                 Make in his mercy retribution.

MERCHANT: Sir, your burgesses and merchant bands
                 Gie thanks to God that we may see your face,
                 Trusting we may now into far-off lands
                 Convey our goods with support of your Grace,
                 For now I trust we shall get rest and peace.
                 When rascals are with your sword overthrown,
                 Then loyal merchants live by trade alone.

CORRECTION: My tender friends, I pray you with my heart,
                 Declare to me and tell me without fear –
                 What is the reason that you go backward?
                 The truth of this is what I want to hear.

BISHOP: Sovereign, we have gone this way mony a year.
                 And although you think we go not decently,
                 We think we make our way right pleasantly.

DILIGENCE: Sit doun, my Lords, into your proper places,
                 And let the King consider all fit cases.

KING HUMANITY: My prudent lords of all the Thrie Estaites,
                 It is our will above all other thing
                 For to reform all them that mak debates
                 Against the truth, which every day they bring,
                 And them that do the Common-weil doun fling.

With help and counsel of King Correction,
It is our will to punish wrong-doing
And on oppressors take our retribution.

BISHOP: What thing is this, Sir, that ye have devised?
Sirs, ye have need for to be well advised!
Be not hasty in your execution,
And be not ower extreme in retribution!
And if you please to do, Sir, as we say,
Postpone this Parliament till another day.
For why? The people of this region
Will not endure extreme correction.

CORRECTION: Is this the part, my lords, that ye will tak –
Not backing us when correction we would mak?
It does appear that ye are culpable
That are not to correction amenable.
Now, Diligence, go show it is our will
That every man oppressed table a bill.

Scene 25: The entrance of Jane the Common-weil

DILIGENCE: All manner of men I warn that be oppressed,
Come and complain, and they shall be redressed.
For now it is the noble Prince's will
That each complainer shall present a bill.

JANE: *(Emerging from the crowd)*
Let me go through! For God's sake, out my way!
Tell me again, good maister, what ye say!

DILIGENCE: I warn all that be wrongfully offended,
Come and complain, and they shall be amended.

JANE: Thanks be to Christ that bore the croon of thorn,
For I was never sae blyth since I was born!

CORRECTION: Tell me your name forthwith I now command.

JANE: I am Jane the Common-weil of fair Scotland.

CORRECTION: Aye, then the Common-weil's seen better days!

JANE: Aye, Sir, that's how the Common-weil wants claes.

CORRECTION: What is the cause the Common-weil is crookit?

JANE: Because the Common-weil has been owerlookit.

CORRECTION: What makes ye look so with a dreary heart?

JANE: Because the Thrie Estaites gang all backward!

CORRECTION: So, Common-weil, know ye the liars that them leads?

JANE: Their canker colours, I ken them by their heids.
As for our reverent fathers of Spirituality,
They are led by Flattery to indulge in gross carnality.
And look, here's Falsehood, and Deceit, weel I ken,
Leaders of the merchants and the silly craftsmen.
What marvel that the Thrie Estaites backward gang
When such a vile company dwells them amang,
Which has ruled the roost here mony dear days,
And made Jane the Common-weil want for claes?
Sir, call them before you and put them in order,
Or else Jane the Common-weil must beg at the border.
You, feigned Flattery! The Fiend fart in your face!

In your guidance to the Court we got little grace!
Rise up, Falsehood and Deceit, weave not your web,
I pray God or the Devil's dame shite on your neb!
Behold how the loon looks even like a thief –
Many a good workman you brought to mischief!
My Sovereign Lord Correction, I mak you supplication.
Put these tried trickers from Christ's congregation!

CORRECTION: As you have devised it, but doubt it shall be so.
Come here, my sergeants, take these rogues and go,
Put all these scoundrels in yer stocks strang –
And later, if ye hang them, ye dae them nae wrang!

1ST SERGEANT: Sovereign Lord, we shall obey your commands.
Fellow, upon these liars lay on your hands.

While Flattery hides in the Spiritual Estaite, the Sergeants take hold of Falsehood and Deceit and put them in the stocks.

2ND SERGEANT: Come here, ye rascal ye, come here, come here!
Yer reckless life ye shall repent.
Don't think that ye can disappear.
Sit still and be obedient!

1ST SERGEANT: Put yer legs into the stocks,
For ye had never better trews.
Sit there while we turn the locks.
Yer liberty it's time tae lose.

Scene 26: The Debate

TEMPORALITY: My Lords, ye know the Thrie Estaites
For Common-weil should mak debates.
Let now amang us be devised
Such acts that by good men be prized.
And so that rumours none hear tell,
Then Diligence, fetch us Guid Counsel,
For she's the very one that knows
Baith the Canon and Civil Laws.

DILIGENCE: *(to Guid Counsel)*
Guid Counsel, ye must with sure intent
Address the Lords of Parliament.

GUID COUNSEL: My Lords, God bless this company!
What is the cause ye send for me?

MERCHANT: Bide here and give us your counsel
To help the poor folk. Now pray tell.
Here, Common-weil, come, have no fear
Let nane except yourself come near.

JANE: *(Bringing the Poor Man out of the crowd)*
Ye must let this puir wranged creature
Support me in this to be sure.
I know his worth full certainly,
He will complain as well as me.

GUID COUNSEL: The common folk do daily, as ye see,
Decline down into extreme poverty.
And now begins a plague amang them new
That gentlemen their steadings tak in feu.

So must they pay great rent or lose their steid,
And some are simply dragged out by the heid,
And are destroyed unless God give in lieu.

POOR MAN: Sir, by God's breid, that tale is very true!
It is weel kenned they took my horse and coos,
Now all I own I wear – nae mair I'd lose.

CORRECTION: Ere I depart I think to make good order.

JANE: I pray you, Sir, begin first at the border.
For how can we defend against England
When we can not within our native land
Destroy each and every Scottish traitor thief
That does to loyal labourers every day mischief?

TEMPORALITY: What other enemy have you? Let us ken.

JANE: Sir, I complain upon the idle men.
For why Sir? It is God's ain bidding
All Christian men to work for their living.
This goes against the strang beggars,
Fiddlers, pipers and pardoners,
The jugglers, jesters and idle ramblers,
The alchemists and chancy gamblers,
The bauble-bearers and their bards,
The spineless spongers, the lords and lairds.
This goes against the great fat friars,
Augustines, Carmelites and holy liars,
And all the rest with tonsured head,
That labour not and are weil fed –
These men not labouring spiritually,
Nor for their living physically,

Lying in dens like idle dogs,
I them compare to weil-fed hogs.
A hundred mair I micht declare,
But to my purpose I'll be fair,
Concluding slothful idleness
Against the Common-weil express.

CORRECTION: Against whom mair will ye complain?

JANE: My God! On mair and mair again!
For the poor people cry with care
At grave injustice everywhere.
Some poor wee petty thief is hanged,
But he that all the world has wranged,
A cruel tyrant, a strang transgressor,
A common public plain oppressor,
Bribes his way, obtaining favours,
And gets off lightly by his labours,
And through laws consistorial
Prolix, corrupt and partial,
The common people are so put under,
That they be poor it is nae wonder.

CORRECTION: Good Jane, I grant all that is true –
Your misfortune full sair I rue.
Before I leave this nation
I shall mak reformation.
And so, my Lord Temporality,
I you command from now that ye
Retain not Falsehood in your lands.
Also I say to you, Merchants,
If ever I find by land or sea
Deceit still in your company,

Which is to Common-weil contrair,
I vow to God I shall not spare
To put my sword to execution,
And on you take full retribution.

TEMPORALITY: So be it, Sir, as long as ye
Treat likewise Spirituality.

CORRECTION: My Spiritual Lords, are ye content?

BISHOP: Na, na, we maun tak advisement.
In such matters for to conclude
Ower hastily we think not good.

CORRECTION: If you conclude not with the Common-weil,
You shall be punished, by good Saint Geil.

BISHOP: Sir, we can show we are exempt
Frae your temporal punishment,
As we would purpose to debate.

CORRECTION: For shame! This is a sorry state.
(To Temporality and Merchant)
My Lords, what say ye to this, pray?

TEMPORALITY: My Sovereign Lord, we will obey
And tak your part with heart and hand,
Whatever ye please us to command.

MERCHANT: But we beseech you, Lord, we pray,
For all our crimes of yesterday
To give us full remission,
And here we will with your permission

The Common-weil for to defend
From henceforth till our lives do end.

CORRECTION: On that condition I am content
To pardon you, since you repent.
The Common-weil tak by the hand
And mak now peace throughout the land.
*(Temporality and the Merchant embrace Jane
the Common-weil.)*
Jane, have ye ony mair debates
Against the Lords of Spiritual states?

JANE: Sir, I'd be sorry if I spoke –
To clype on priests is no a joke!

CORRECTION: Flyte away! I'll think it not uncouth –
Tell the truth and nothing but the truth.

JANE: Thank you, Sir, then I'll no haud back,
On the Bishop complaint I'll mak.
The poor cottar being like to die,
Having young infants twa or three,
And his twa coos – he has nae mair –
The Bishop takes one – it's no fair –
Wi the grey quilt that covers the bed,
Although the wife be poorly cled.
And if the wife die on the morn,
Though all the bairns should be forlorn,
The other cow he cleiks away
Wi the poor coat of rapploch grey.
Pray God this custom were confounded –
It never was on reason founded!

TEMPORALITY: Are all the tales true that she tells?

POOR MAN: True, sir, the Devil stick me else!
For by the Haily Trinity,
The same thing has been done to me!

JANE: Our bishops wi their lusty robes of white,
They flow in riches, royalty and delight.
Like Paradise are their palaces and places,
And want nae pleasure of the fairest faces.

POOR MAN: All these prelates have great prerogatives,
And constantly they walk oot on their wives,
And tak up wi some whoor ootside marriage
And run like rams rudely in their rage,
Their pizzles oot among the silly yows,
As lang as sap their randy natures rouse.

PARSON: You lie, false whoor and ragged loon!
There is nae priest in all this toon
That is so wanton in his job.

JANE: The Fiend will shut your lying gob!

BISHOP: My Lords, why do ye thole that loathsome loon
And let him honest kirk-men so put doon?
Yon villain puts me out of charity!

TEMPORALITY: Why, my Lord, speaks he ought but verity?

BISHOP: I will not suffer the words of yon villain.

POOR MAN: Then give me back my three fat coos again!

BISHOP: False cur! Before me stand you not in awe?

POOR MAN: The Fiend receive them that first devised that law!

BISHOP: I mak a vow, these words ye shall repent!

CORRECTION: I tell you now, my Lords, be patient.
We came here nocht for disputations –
We came to mak guid reformations.

MERCHANT: My Lord, conclude that all the temporal lands
Be set in feu to labourers with their hands.

CORRECTION: My Lord Bishop, will you thereto consent?

BISHOP: Na! Na! Never till the Day of Judgement!

TEMPORALITY: My Lord, by Him that all the world has wrought,
We care not whether ye consent or not –
Ye are but one Estaite and we are twa.
Who has the greater part here has it aa!

JANE: If I were king, sir, by Christ's Passion,
I would go make a proclamation
That never a penny should go to Rome at all,
Nae mair than did to Peter nor to Paul.

MERCHANT: My Lord, I think it best, it's my advice,
That priest and church should profit not frae vice.

GUID COUNSEL: A bishop's office is for to be a preacher
And of the Law of God a public teacher!

BISHOP: And where find ye that we should preachers be?

GUID COUNSEL: Look what Saint Paul writes unto Timothy.
Tak there the book. Let's see if you can spell!

BISHOP: I never read that, therefore read it yoursel!

GUID COUNSEL: Sit still, my Lord, there's no need for to brawl –
These are the very words o the Apostle Paul.

BISHOP: Some say, by Him that wore the croon of thorn,
It had been best had Paul never been born.

GUID COUNSEL: But ye must know, my Lord, Saint Paul's intent.
Sir, read ye never the New Testament?

BISHOP: Na, sir, by him that our Lord Jesus sold,
I never read New Testament nor Old,
Nor ever think to do so, by the Rood –
I hear friars say that reading does nae good.

TEMPORALITY: Then before God, how can ye be excusit,
To hold an office and know not how to use it?

MERCHANT: Ye say that to the Apostles ye succeed
But ye show it not in either word or deed.

JANE: And out of Heaven, what if God looked doon
And saw the great abomination
Among their abbeys and their nunneries
Their public whoordoms and their harlotries?

PRIORESS: How dare you, cur, presume so to declare,
             Or meddle in such matters? Say nae mair!
             If you don't haud yer wheesht, then mark it well,
             I tell you that you'll be condemned to Hell!

PARSON: My Lord Bishop, I marvel how that ye
             Suffer this churl for to speak heresy,
             For by my faith, my Lord, hear what I say,
             She deserves for to be burnt here straight away.

BISHOP: Haily Faither, examine there that bitch.
             Show forth her faith. Let's see if she's a witch.
             Then to the Lord my God a vow I'll take –
             That this bastard shall be burned here at the stake!

FLATTERY: Venerable father, I shall do your command,
             If she deserves death, I shall soon understand.
             (To Jane)
             False whoor and hag, show forth thy faith!

JANE: I think ye speak but as a wraith!
             To you I have naething to say –
             You're no my priest, now go away!

FLATTERY: Say who's yer God, false monster fanged?

JANE: My God is He who'll see you hanged!
             (to Correction)
             Sir, will you give me audience
             And I shall show your Excellence,
             If now your Grace may give me leave,
             How in the Lord God I believe?

CORRECTION: Show forth your faith, and feign ye not.

JANE: I believe in God, that all has wrought
Creating every thing of nought,
And in His Son, our Lord Jesu,
Incarnate of the Virgin true,
Who under Pilate tholed the passion,
And died for mankind's sure salvation,
And on the third day rose again,
As holy scripture shows us plain.
Also, my Lord, it is weil kenned
How He did unto Heaven ascend,
And set Him doon at the richt hand
Of God the Father, I understand,
And shall come to judge us on Doomsday.
What will ye mair, Sir, that I say?

CORRECTION: Show forth the rest. In your soul, search.

JANE: I believe too in the sanctity of the Church –
But nocht in these bishops or their priests
Wha copulate like whoorson beasts!

CORRECTION: Say what ye will, sirs, by Saint Ann,
I think Jane is a good Christian.

Scene 27: The expulsion of Sprituality

Verity and Chastity come forward.

VERITY: My Sovereign, I beseech your Excellence,
Use justice upon Spirituality,

                  For he has done to us great violence
                  And put us close into captivity.

CHASTITY: My Lord, I have great cause for to complain –
                  I could nae lodging get here in this land,
                  The Prioress held me in such disdain.
                  For with Dame Sensual she went hand in hand.

CORRECTION: What say ye now, my lady Prioress?
                  How have ye used your office? Now confess
                  What was the cause ye refused sanctuary
                  To this young lusty lady, Chastity?

PRIORESS: I would have harboured her with good intent
                  But my temperament thereto would not assent.
                  My use of office is my ain concern –
                  Speak to my friar if mair ye needs must learn!

GUID COUNSEL: Yon prioress, it is nae fable,
                  I think she is not profitable
                  And sic like friars in every region
                  The Common-weil put to confusion.
                  Please you dismiss them out of hand
                  And banish them from out this land.

1ST SERGEANT: *(To Correction)*
                  Sir, please you that we two restrain them,
                  And, at your pleasure, we'll detain them
                  Prior tae banishment.

CORRECTION: Pass on – I am richt weil content
                  And to this action give consent.
                  It is fit punishment.

FLATTERY: Now what is this the monster means?
               We are exempt frae kings and queens
               And frae all human law!

2ND SERGEANT: Tak ye the hood and I the gown –
               This ligger looks as like a clown
               As any I ever saw!

The Sergeants grab Flattery and divest him of his friar's habit.

GUID COUNSEL: Sir, by the Holy Trinity,
               This same is feigning Flattery –
               I ken him by his face.
               Believing he would get promotion,
               He said that his name was Devotion,
               And so beguiled your Grace.

2ND SERGEANT: Come, Lady Prioress,
               We'll learn ye how tae dance,
               And step wi nae distress,
               A new pavane frae France!

They grab the Prioress and pull off her habit, revealing a silk dress underneath.

1ST SERGEANT: I dinnae need tae guess,
               By my judgement I'm sure
               This haily Prioress
               Has turned intae a whoor!

PRIORESS: My curses upon every one
               That did compel me be a nun
               And wouldnae let me marry.
               It was my family's greediness

That made me be a Prioress
So they should pay nae dowry.
Howbeit that nuns sing nicht and day,
Their hearts feel nocht what their mooths say,
And so the truth it runs.
Now here I gie ye intimation
Tae all within Christ's congregation –
There is nae need for nuns.
But I shall dae the best I can,
And marry some guid honest man,
And with ill ways be done.
Marriage, I am glad tae say,
Is better religion ony day
Than being a friar or nun.

FLATTERY: My Lords, for God's sake do not hang me,
Although that gallows-bird would wrang me!
For I shall help to hang my fellows.

CORRECTION: Then pass by and prepare the gallows!
(Dismisses him)
With the advice of King Humanity
Here I determine with ripe advisement
That all these prelates deprived shall be,
As is decreed by this present Parliament.
(Indicating Guid Counsel, Verity and Chastity)
Then these three shining Virtues heaven sent
Immediately their places shall possess,
Because that they have been sae negligent
Suffering the Word of God such great distress.

KING HUMANITY: As ye have said, doubt not it shall be done –
Pass to and interchange them every one.

The King's servants approach Spirituality and the Parson.

WANTONNESS: My Lords, we pray you patience tae tak tent
For we are carrying out the King's commandment.

BISHOP: I make a vow to God, if us you handle,
You shall be cursed with bell and book and candle!

The prelates are seized and replaced by Guid Counsel, Verity and Chastity. The prelates' robes are removed; revealing motley underneath.

JANE: We marvel at you, painted sepulchres,
Accepting you has been a very curse.
With glorious habit you rode upon your mules,
Now men may see you are but very fools!

BISHOP: We say the Kings were greater fools than we,
That us promoted to great dignity.

PARSON: There is a thousand in the kirk, don't doubt,
Such fools as we, if they were weil sought out.

BISHOP: I see nocht else, my brother, without fail,
But this false world is turned frae top tae tail,
And everything is vain that's under Heaven –
Tae eat we'll have tae go and earn a livin.

The Bishop, the Parson and the Prioress are escorted off.

Scene 28: The garbing of Jane

GUID COUNSEL: My Lord, before you go forth frae this toon,
Give Jane the Common-weil a bright new goon.
For sake of profit she has been sore suppressed,
Leaving her cold, ragged and ill-dressed.

CORRECTION: As ye have said, Guid Counsel, I'm content –
Let Jane a fine new garment now be sent,
Of satin, velvet, or of silk replete
And let her in our Parliament take a seat.

They clothe Jane gorgeously and set her down among them in the Parliament. During this, Divine Correction disappears.

POOR MAN: This noble deed, I understand,
Will bring great honour to Scotland.
But I beseech you, on the gallows
To hang Deceit and sic like fellows,
And banish Flattery oot this toon,
For there was never such a loon!

KING HUMANITY: As you have said, so shall it be.
Now string them up for all to see!

Scene 29: The hanging of the Vices

The Sergeants move towards Falsehood and Deceit, who are being led this way by Flattery.

DECEIT: Now, my auld friend Flattery,
What's said by King Humanity?

FLATTERY: You'll baith be hanged, I'm sorry to say,
            Strung up yonder straight away.

DECEIT: The Fiend flay ye! So now they'll hang us?
            The Deil brought yon cursed king amang us!

FLATTERY: I'd have been put to death amang you,
            Had I not took on hand to hang you.

2ND SERGEANT: Come here, Deceit, we'll ding ye doon!
                Saw ever man a likelier loon
                To hang upon a gallows?

DECEIT: Now I am wracked, with sorrow wrung –
            To think that I should end up hung!
            Let me speak with my fellows.

1ST SERGEANT: Come here, Falsehood, and grace the gallows,
                Ye must hang here before your fellows
                For your cankered condition!
                Many a true man have ye wranged,
                So without doubt ye shall be hanged –
                Nae mercy or remission!

FALSEHOOD: Alas, must I be hanged here too?
            What muckle devil made this true?
            How came I to this station?
            My guid maisters, renowned Craftsmen,
            Without Falsehood, full weil I ken,
            Ye will die of starvation!

DECEIT: Adieu, my maisters, Merchant men –
            I've served ye well, as fine ye ken,
            In truth, till you're replete.

I say to you, in due conclusion,
I dreid you'll all gang tae confusion
Without your friend Deceit!

2ND SERGEANT: Enough, man, of your clitter-clatter!

DECEIT: For God's sake, pray let me mak watter!

1ST SERGEANT: *(to Falsehood)*
Now, in this halter slip your heid!

FALSEHOOD: Alas, guid woman, ye want me deid!

DECEIT: Adieu! I tell ye all – Hell mend!

FALSEHOOD: Falsehood never made a better end!

Flattery knocks out the counterweight on the ropes with a large
hammer so that Falsehood and Deceit are strung up.

FLATTERY: Have I nocht struck the gallows well?
Aye, that I have, and lived to tell!
My death-knell hasnae rung.
For I deserved here, by All Hallows,
To have been strung up with my fellows,
And high above them hung!
I made far mair faults than my mates,
I beguiled all the Thrie Estaites
With my hypocrisy.
When I had on my friar's hood
All men believed that I was good –
Now judge ye if I be!
What holiness is there within

A wolf clad in a sheep's clothin?
Adieu! I'll cross the watter,
And gang awa tae distant lands
Tae seek fresh fools on far flung strands
And teach them how tae flatter!

Scene 30: Folly's sermon

As Flattery runs out, Folly enters.

FOLLY: Good day, my Lords, and God bless you!
Does no man bid Good day the noo?
When fools are fou, they're fine, it's true!
Ken ye not me?
How call they me, can ye not tell?
Now, by Him that has harried Hell,
I don't know what they call mysel,
Or who I be!

DILIGENCE: What rogue is this maks such a rammy?

FOLLY: Who's asking, pal? I doubt you're bammy!
Away ye go, run tae yer mammy
Wi muck upon yer mow!

DILIGENCE: Daft fool, what's got ye in such a state?

FOLLY: It's they traffic lights in the Bonnygate.
And then there was a great debate
Between me and a sow.
The sow's great guff it made me greet,
I got away, fast on my feet,

But in the middle of the street
I fell into a midden.
'Hello fair midden!' I ken, I ken!
She sat on me wi her rear end –
I curse the Cooncil that streets should mend!
And that should be God's bidding.

KING HUMANITY: Pass on, my servant Diligence,
And bring that fool to our presence.

DILIGENCE: Folly, come without tarrying –
Ye must stand here before the King.

FOLLY: The King? What kind of thing is that?
Is he the one wi the golden hat?

DILIGENCE: The very same, come on your way.

FOLLY: If ye be King, God give ye good day –
I've a complaint to make right now!

KING HUMANITY: Against whom, Folly?

FOLLY: A stupid sow!
Sir, she has sworn that she will slay me
Or else bite baith my bollocks frae me!
If you will not mak due correction,
Then give unto me your protection
Against all swine give me redress,
Between this town and Inverness!

DILIGENCE: Get up, Folly, no tarrying!
And speed you hastily to the King.
Get up! I think the churl is dumb!

FOLLY: Now bum balerie, bum, bum, bum!
          (Spying the audience)
          Oh, whit a comely congregation!
          Are ye come tae hear some great oration?
          (Realising audience is looking at him)
          Am I supposed tae dae some preaching?

KING HUMANITY: Now, Folly, let us hear your teaching,
                  To pass our time, let's hear you rave!

FOLLY: As you command, so Christ me save!
          (Launches into sermon)
          Solomon, the wisest King, did write
          The number of fools is infinite.
          (Indicates audience)
          So of the hundreds here you see,
          There may be fools as great as me!
          Because there are so many fools –
          Though some wear fancy clothes and jewels
          I've brought some stuff, to sell I'll try
          To any fool that wants to buy –
          (Produces folly hats out of a basket)
          And specially for the Thrie Estaites,
          Where I have many tender mates,
          Who made them all, as you did see,
          Gang backward through the hail country.

DILIGENCE: Who'd buy this hat? Pray let me ken!

FOLLY: It's made for insatiable Merchant men!
          Though riches are their provenance,
          They're not content and take a chance.
          They sail into the stormy blast
          In winter, wide their nets they'll cast

For profit under great torment,
Against the Acts of Parliament.
Some lose their gear and some are drowned –
With this such Merchants should be crowned!

Folly crowns the Merchant with the hat.

DILIGENCE: Tae whom d'ye mean tae sell that hood?
I think tae some great man of good.

FOLLY: *(Pointing at Temporality)*
I do intend this hood be sold
Unto a man that's old and cold,
Who has seen eighty years of life
And taks a lass tae be his wife,
A fifth the age that he is now
When they baith tak their marriage vow,
Trusting she's no one o they bitches
Who'd hae affairs and keep his riches.
Who marries thus when nearly deid,
Set this hat upon his heid!

Folly crowns Temporality with the hat.

DILIGENCE: What hood is that? Tell me I pray ye.

FOLLY: This is a holy hat I say ye.
It's been ordained, I tell ye true,
For spiritual fools – I've seen a few!
Others' souls tae save it suits them weil –
They sell their ain souls to the Deil!
Whoever does so, this I conclude,
Upon his heid let him set this false hood!

DILIGENCE: Folly, are there ony such men
                Here in the Kirk that ye dae ken?

FOLLY: I darenae pick fae the prelacy –
                I micht get burnt for heresy!

KING HUMANITY: Speak on, Folly, I give you leave.

FOLLY: Then my remission is in my sleeve!
                (He crowns Guid Counsel with the hat.)
                Will ye let me now speak of Kings?

KING HUMANITY: Go on, speak of all kind of things!

FOLLY: Conforming to my first narration,
                I say you're all fools, by Christ's Passion!

DILIGENCE: You lie! That's madness from your tongue!

FOLLY: If I lie, God or you be hung!
                For I have here, as now I'll tell,
                A noble cap imperial,
                Which is not ordained for sic-like things
                Of emperors and dukes and kings,
                For princely and imperial fools –
                They should have lugs as lang as mules!
                (He exchanges headgear with the King.)
                The pride of princes all without fail
                Make the hail world run top over tail.
                To win them worldly good and glory,
                They shed men's blood, their hands are gory.
                They learned not this at Christ's good schools,
                Therefore I think them very fools.

Now of my sermon I have made an end.
To Billy Connolly I ye all commend!

Folly exits. The King has been uncomfortable, but now laughs. Diligence comes forward.

DILIGENCE: Now let ilk man his way advance,
Let some gae drink and some gae dance.
Minstrel, blow up a brawl of France –
Let's see who hobbles best!
For I will run fast, noo tak tent,
Unto the tavern for merriment,
And pray to God omnipotent
To send you all good rest.

(THE END)

Appendix: Cast breakdown
(First half of Part One)

> X: Speaking during the scene
> O: Silent but involved in scene
> *: Onstage watching

Scene numbers:	1	2	3	4	5	6	7	8	9	10
DILIGENCE	X	*	*	*	*	*	*	*	*	*
KING HUMANITY	X	X	*	X	*	X	X			X
WANTONNESS	X	X	*	X	X	X	X			X
CHILL-OOT	X	X	*	X	*	O	O			O
SANDY SOLACE	X	X	*	X	X	O	O			X
SENSUALITY			X	*	X	*	X			O
HAMELINESS			X	*	O	*	X			X
DANGER			X	*	O	*	O			X
JANET			X	*	O	*	O			O
GUID COUNSEL	X							X	*	O
FLATTERY									X	X
FALSEHOOD									X	X
DECEIT									X	X
VERITY	X									
THE BISHOP	X	*	*	*	*	*	*	*	*	*
THE PRIORESS	X	*	*	*	*	*	*	*	*	*
THE PARSON	X	*	*	*	*	*	*	*	*	*
CHASTITY	X									
TEMPORALITY	X	*	*	*	*	*	*	*	*	*
MERCHANT	X	*	*	*	*	*	*	*	*	*
SERGEANTS	X									

Cast breakdown
(Second half of Part One)

| X: Speaking during the scene |
| O: Silent but involved in scene |
| *: Onstage watching |

Scene numbers:	11	12	13	14	15	16	17	18	19	20
DILIGENCE	*	*	*	X	X	*	*	*	*	X
KING HUMANITY	*	X	*	*	X	*	*	*	X	X
WANTONNESS	*	O	*	*	O	*	*	*	X	X
CHILL-OOT	*	O	*	*	O	*	*	*	X	X
SANDY SOLACE	*	X	*	*	X	*	*	*	X	X
SENSUALITY	*	X	*	*	X	*	*	*	X	
HAMELINESS	*	X	*	*	O	*	*	*	O	
DANGER	*	X	*	*	O	*	*	*	O	
JANET	*	X	*	*	O	*	*	*	O	
GUID COUNSEL	X	*	*	*	*	*	*	X	O	X
FLATTERY	X	X	X	*	X	*	X	*	*	*
FALSEHOOD	X	O	O	*	O	*	X	*	*	*
DECEIT	X	O	X	*	O	*	X	*	*	*
VERITY			X	*	X	*	*	O	O	X
SPIRITUALITY	*	*	X	X	*	*	*	*	X	*
THE PRIORESS	*	*	X	X	*	*	*	*	O	*
THE PARSON	*	*	X	X	*	*	*	*	O	*
CHASTITY				X	X	*	*	X	O	X
TEMPORALITY	*	*	*	X	*	*	*	*	*	*
MERCHANT	*	*	*	X	*	*	*	*	*	*
SOUTAR				X						
TAYLOR				X						
JENNY TAYLOR				X						
MRS TAYLOR				X						
MRS SOUTAR				X						
VARLET						X				
CORRECTION								X	X	X
SERGEANTS								O	*	*

Cast breakdown
(Part Two)

> X: Speaking during the scene
> O: Silent but involved in scene
> *: Onstage watching

Scene numbers:	21	22	23	24	25	26	27	28	29	30
DILIGENCE	X	*	O	X	X	X	*	*	*	X
KING HUMANITY				X	O	O	X	X	*	X
WANTONNESS				X	*	*	X	O	*	O
CHILL-OOT				X	*	*	O	O	*	O
SANDY SOLACE				X	*	*	O	O	*	O
GUID COUNSEL				X	*	X	X	X	*	O
FLATTERY		X	X	O	O	X	X	*	X	
FALSEHOOD				O	O	*	*	*	X	
DECEIT				O	O	*	*	*	X	
VERITY				O	*	*	X	O	*	O
THE BISHOP				X	*	X	X			
THE PRIORESS	*	*	*	O	*	X	X			
THE PARSON	*	*	*	O	*	X	X			
CHASTITY				O	*	*	X	O	*	O
TEMPORALITY				X	*	X	*	O	*	O
MERCHANT				X	*	X	*	O	*	O
SOUTAR		X								
MRS SOUTAR		X								
CORRECTION				X	X	X	X	X		
POOR MAN	X	*	X	*	*	X	*	X	*	O
JANE					X	X	X	X	*	O
SERGEANTS				*	X	O	X	O	X	O
FOLLY										X

Weapons and Technology of
World War II

Windsor Chorlton

www.heinemann.co.uk
Visit our website to find out more information about Heinemann Library books.

To order:
☎ Phone 44 (0) 1865 888066
▤ Send a fax to 44 (0) 1865 314091
▢ Visit the Heinemann Bookshop at www.heinemann.co.uk to browse our catalogue
and order online.

First published in Great Britain by Heinemann Library,
Halley Court, Jordan Hill, Oxford OX2 8EJ,
a division of Reed Educational and Professional Publishing Ltd.
Heinemann is a registered trademark of Reed Educational and Professional Publishing Ltd.

OXFORD MELBOURNE AUCKLAND
JOHANNESBURG BLANTYRE GABORONE
IBADAN PORTSMOUTH (NH) USA CHICAGO

Produced for Heinemann Library by Discovery Books Limited
Designed by Sabine Beaupré
Illustrations by Mark Franklin
Maps by Stefan Chabluk
Consultant: Stewart Ross
Originated by Dot Gradations
Printed by Wing King Tong in Hong Kong

ISBN 0 431 11996 1 (hardback)   ISBN 0 431 12001 3 (paperback)
06 05 04 03   06 05 04 03
10 9 8 7 6 5 4 3 2   10 9 8 7 6 5 4 3 2 1

British Library Cataloguing in Publication Data
Chorlton, Windsor 1948–
  Weapons and technology of World War II. – (20th century perspectives)
  1. World War, 1939–1945 – Equipment and supplies – Juvenile literature
  I. Title
  623.4'09044

Acknowledgements
The publishers would like to thank the following for permission to reproduce photographs:
Corbis, pp. 4, 6, 7, 13, 14, 15, 16, 17, 18, 19, 20, 22, 24, 25, 30, 31, 32, 35 (top and bottom),
36, 37, 38, 39, 40, 41, 42, 43; Hulton Getty, pp. 9; 27, 28, 29 (bottom), 33, 34; Peter Newark's
Pictures, pp. 8, 10, 11, 26, 29 (top).

Cover photograph reproduced with permission of Corbis.

Every effort has been made to contact copyright holders of any material reproduced in this book.
Any omissions will be rectified in subsequent printings if notice is given to the publishers.

Any words appearing in the text in bold, **like this**, are explained in the glossary.

Contents

Hitler on the warpath

Military build-up

In World War One, which raged from 1914 to 1918 on battlefronts in Europe and beyond, Germany and its allies had been defeated. After its defeat, Germany signed the Treaty of Versailles with some of the victorious nations – Italy, France and Britain. Under this agreement, Germany was allowed only a small army, a tiny navy and no air force at all.

But when Adolf Hitler, the leader of the Nazi party, came to power in 1933, he immediately set about rearming Germany. His long-term aim was to carve out a German **empire** in the Soviet Union. The other European nations began to rearm, too, but took no direct action to stop Hitler. In 1939, the Soviet leader Josef Stalin signed a non-aggression pact with Hitler, hoping it would buy him time to build up his own armed forces.

Adolf Hitler (seen here at a Nazi party rally) and the Nazis were fascists, which means they believed in complete control of society by government. They also thought their race was superior to others.

Lightning war

Under Hitler, Germany would wage a new type of warfare. *Blitzkrieg*, meaning 'lightning war', used massed tank formations supported by aeroplanes to rip through enemy defences. The *blitzkrieg* tactic was first used with devastating effect when Germany invaded Poland in September 1939.

A war without limits

Two days after the invasion, Britain and France – known as the Allied Powers, or Allies – declared war on Germany. The next year, Hitler's army invaded and occupied France. Then, in 1941, Germany invaded the Soviet Union, having made an alliance with Japan in the hope that the Japanese would invade the Soviets from the East. Instead, Japan launched a war of expansion in the Pacific (see map on page 21). This started in December 1941 with an attack on the US fleet in Hawaii.

The USA and Canada immediately declared war on Japan. Germany and its main European ally, Italy – which together with Japan were termed the Axis Powers – in turn declared war on the USA. Two years after German tanks rolled across the Polish border, the conflict had become global. World War Two would involve 200 countries before it ended in 1945.

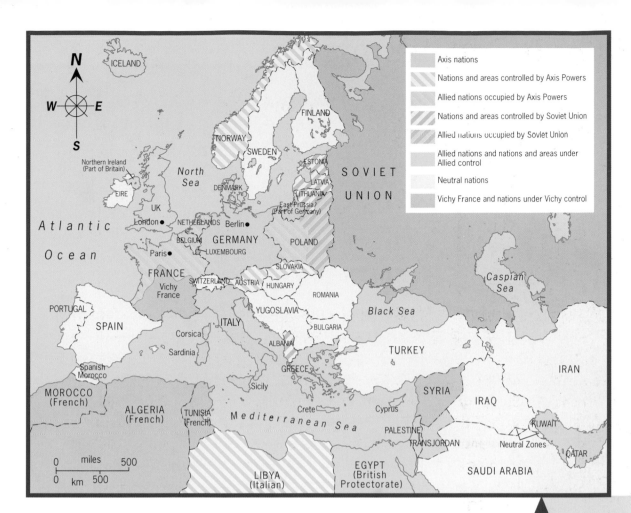

Map legend:
- Axis nations
- Nations and areas controlled by Axis Powers
- Allied nations occupied by Axis Powers
- Nations and areas controlled by Soviet Union
- Allied nations occupied by Soviet Union
- Allied nations and nations and areas under Allied control
- Neutral nations
- Vichy France and nations under Vichy control

Map labels: ICELAND, FINLAND, NORWAY, SWEDEN, ESTONIA, LATVIA, LITHUANIA, Northern Ireland (Part of Britain), North Sea, DENMARK, East Prussia (Part of Germany), SOVIET UNION, EIRE, UK, London, NETHERLANDS, Berlin, Atlantic Ocean, BELGIUM, GERMANY, POLAND, Paris, LUXEMBOURG, SLOVAKIA, FRANCE, SWITZERLAND, AUSTRIA, HUNGARY, Vichy France, ROMANIA, Caspian Sea, PORTUGAL, YUGOSLAVIA, Black Sea, SPAIN, Corsica, ITALY, BULGARIA, ALBANIA, Sardinia, GREECE, TURKEY, IRAN, Spanish Morocco, Sicily, SYRIA, IRAQ, MOROCCO (French), ALGERIA (French), TUNISIA (French), Mediterranean Sea, Crete, Cyprus, KUWAIT, PALESTINE, Neutral Zones, QATAR, TRANSJORDAN, EGYPT (British Protectorate), SAUDI ARABIA, LIBYA (Italian)

Scale: 0 miles 500 / 0 km 500

Powerful weapons

The tanks, aeroplanes and ships of World War Two were not new weapons, but they were faster and more powerfully armed than anything seen before. Radio, **radar** and other **electronic** devices made them deadlier still. Fast-moving tanks communicating by radio could win or lose battles involving millions of men in a matter of days. Long-range bombers guided by radar could navigate at night to targets deep inside enemy territory. Submarines and aircraft carriers made every part of the world a potential battlefield.

World War Two was the first conflict in which scientists made a major contribution. The war was responsible for the development of the jet engine, electronic computers, **antibiotics** and **insecticides**. The period of conflict and the time before it also produced two terrible new weapons, the atomic bomb and the **ballistic missile**.

World War Two was fought on the **home front** as well as on the battlefield. Economic power was as important as military **strategy**, and every available worker was mobilized to produce the weapons and materials that kept the conflict going. As a result, **civilians** as well as soldiers were sometimes seen as military targets.

By 1940, the Axis Powers had control of much of Europe. The Germans had occupied the northern part of France and made the southern region into a separate territory called Vichy France. The areas under control of the Vichy government sided with the Axis Powers.

5

Weapons of the infantry

The brunt of the fighting in World War Two was borne by the **infantry** using mainly **rifles**, machine guns and pistols to kill the enemy or to repel attackers. Most infantrymen carried a rifle, a medium-range gun accurate up to 500 metres. When infantry attacked or retreated, they were protected by covering fire from machine guns that could loose off up to 1000 **rounds** a minute.

Carbines and assault rifles

World War Two produced new types of small weapons that were compromises between the accuracy of a rifle, the portability of a pistol and the firepower of a machine gun. The Americans, for example, sacrificed accuracy for ease of handling with the M1 carbine, a rifle with a short **barrel** weighing little more than 2 kilograms. The Germans produced the MP44, an assault rifle that could fire either a single shot almost as accurately as a rifle, or bursts of fire like a machine gun.

Sub-machine guns

The sub-machine gun, first used at the end of World War One and very popular with American gangsters in the 1920s, was a cross between a pistol and a machine gun. Light enough to be fired in one hand, it could deliver thirty rounds in less than four seconds.

In World War Two, sub-machine guns were used for close combat in confined spaces where firepower counted for more than accuracy. During the battle for the Soviet city of Stalingrad, German soldiers armed with Schmeissers fought from building to building and room to

*An Australian infantry unit practises a **bayonet** charge during training. For direct combat, soldiers had bayonets attached to their rifles so the weapons would double as a spear at close quarters.*

room against Soviet infantry armed with the PPSh-41. The British equivalent was the Sten gun, and American forces used the MIAI Thompson and the M3. All were produced in large numbers. By contrast, the Japanese made only a tiny number of sub-machine guns.

Anti-tank weapons

Another World War Two **innovation** gave infantrymen a fighting chance against armoured vehicles such as tanks. Portable anti-tank weapons fired a special **grenade** that had a front face hollowed out to make a metal-lined cone. When the grenade exploded, it produced a jet of gas and molten metal that could penetrate **armour plating** to a depth of about three times the diameter of the cone. These anti-tank weapons were hazardous to use, however. The British version, the Projector Infantry Anti-Tank (PIAT), was fired by a powerful spring. The **recoil** was supposed to re-set the spring for the next shot, but it often failed to work. The gunner, lying behind the gun, would then have to stand up to reload, exposing himself to enemy fire.

Land-mines, used as anti-tank and anti-vehicle weapons, were horribly dangerous for infantry and **civilians**. They were cases filled with explosives and laid in the ground, where they exploded when disturbed. Their most extensive use was in the deserts of North Africa, where there were few natural barriers and the enemy might attack from any direction. An estimated 18 million unexploded World War Two land-mines remain in Egypt's Western Desert.

*An American soldier keeps watch with a portable anti-tank weapon. The bazooka (seen here), and the similar German panzerfaust, fired **rocket**-propelled grenades. The rocket spewed out flame as it left the barrel, making it dangerous for the user.*

Mobile infantry

German infantry were transported by trucks or vehicles fitted with tracks that enabled them to travel across rough country. The mobility of these forces was demonstrated at the start of Germany's 1941 invasion of the Soviet Union, when the attackers advanced 660 km (410 m) in three weeks. The Allied armies adopted similar measures. Armies also used small, sturdy vehicles for **reconnaissance** and carrying messages. The USA turned out so many four-wheel-drive Jeeps (from 'GPs' or 'general purpose' vehicles) that they became a common mode of transport on all battlefronts.

Artillery

World War One had seen the use of huge heavy guns, or **artillery**, capable of firing **shells** more than 15 kilometres (9 miles). Their attacks on enemy positions were made safely from several kilometres behind the **front lines**. This system was useless against the more mobile targets of World War Two, however. To destroy fast-moving tanks and motorized **infantry**, gunners had to get within visual range. This meant using light artillery pieces that could be moved quickly from place to place.

Mortars are a type of portable artillery used by infantry. Mortars fire shells high rather than far, and so they are effective at close range against enemy positions hidden behind hills or buildings. **Howitzers**, another form of artillery, varied from heavy guns to small, portable versions. The 75 millimetre pack howitzer could break down into parts small enough to be delivered in rough terrain by parachute.

Whether light or heavy, all artillery fired shells of one kind or another. The shells were metal cases containing explosives that caused extensive damage when they exploded on reaching their target. In some cases, the US army used a radio-controlled **fuse** that **detonated** an artillery shell in the air directly above its target, making it up to twenty times more effective than a shell that exploded on or in the ground.

Allied soldiers load shells into an anti-tank gun during the capture of the French town of St Malo in 1944.

The 88

The most famous artillery weapon of World War Two was the German 88 millimetre. Designed as an anti-aircraft gun, the 88 was pressed into service as an anti-tank weapon during the battle for France in 1940. It was also used with great success against Allied tanks in North Africa from 1940 to 1943. The 88 was one of the few weapons that proved effective against Soviet T-34 tanks. From 2000 metres away, a single shell from an 88 could penetrate **armour plating** 100 millimetres thick. While most artillery pieces were in a fixed position between two wheels, the 88 could be smoothly rotated on a platform to fire in any direction.

Self-propelled artillery and rockets

The 88 was light enough to be transported on a truck, but it was not a true mobile weapon. The Germans pioneered self-propelled artillery and it was later taken up by the British and Americans. These weapons were capable of keeping up with tanks, as they were adapted tanks themselves, fitted with high-**velocity** guns. The vehicles, such as the German Jagdtiger which carried a 128 millimetre gun, were heavily armoured to protect the gun crew. Unlike tanks, however, self-propelled artillery had guns that pointed straight ahead, making them vulnerable to attacks from the rear.

The Germans and Soviets also developed battlefield **rocket** launchers that fired gas-propelled missiles armed with explosive **warheads**. The German Nebelwerfer fired six rockets at two-second intervals. Allied troops who encountered it in France called it the 'screaming meanie' for the eerie sound of the incoming rockets.

Rocket launchers were one kind of artillery used in the Battle of Kursk in 1943. The vehicle-mounted Soviet Katyusha, seen here, fired up to 48 rockets from a multiple launcher that was known as a 'Stalin organ'.

Artillery barrages

When a **stalemate** was reached, massed artillery could be used to initiate new assaults. The 900-gun **barrage** with which the British launched the 1942 Battle of El Alamein in North Africa was the heaviest since 1918. During the Battle of Kursk in 1943, 26,000 Soviet artillery pieces fired 42 million **rounds**. In the 1945 Battle for Berlin, the Soviets packed up to 640 guns into each kilometre of their front line. **Civilians** were often victims of artillery barrages. The besieged Soviet citizens of Leningrad endured more than two years of German shelling before the Soviet army relieved the city.

Tanks

Tanks, with their combination of mobility, powerful guns and thick armour, proved to be the main **offensive** land weapon of World War Two, except in the Far East. Their **caterpillar tracks** enabled them to cross ground impassable by wheeled vehicles. Their guns could rotate to fire **shells** in any direction at enemy tanks or **strongpoints**.

Blitzkrieg

Before the war began, most armies believed that the role of tanks was limited to supporting **infantry** movements. It was the Germans who first adopted the tactic of using tanks backed up by aircraft, **artillery** and infantry to lead all-out assaults.

The invasion of Poland in 1939 was a one-sided contest in which defending infantry stood no chance against Germany's *blitzkrieg*. The Germans' tanks, called panzers, that invaded Poland faced a tougher

In 1941 Germany launched the huge Operation Barbarossa against the Soviet Union. The armoured divisions, including thousands of panzers such as these, led the invasion.

test the next year in France, the Netherlands and Belgium. There they were outnumbered by Allied tanks. However, the Allies' tanks were spread out along the entire front. The main panzer force attacked through the hilly, forested land of the Belgian Ardennes, which the French mistakenly thought was impassable by tanks. Bypassing enemy strongpoints, the panzers reached the French coast in eleven days.

That's what I need! That's what I want!

Adolf Hitler after seeing tanks demonstrated in 1933.

Tanks on the Eastern Front

It wasn't until Germany invaded the Soviet Union in 1941 that the panzers met their match. The Soviet T–34 tank had a high-**velocity** gun that could destroy a panzer before the German tank could get in range with its own gun. Its wide tracks enabled it to cross rough or boggy ground that would bring a panzer to a halt. Shells often glanced harmlessly off its sloping **armour plating**.

Panthers and Tigers

The Germans soon incorporated many of the T-34's features in their Panther, widely regarded as the best battle tank of the war. Armed with a 75-millimetre long-range gun, the four-man Panther had armour up to 60 millimetres thick that couldn't be penetrated by the Allies' main anti-tank weapons. Although it weighed 45 tonnes, it had a top speed of 54 kilometres per hour (34 miles per hour).

The Germans also built two giant tanks, the Tiger I and Tiger II, both armed with 88 millimetre guns that could destroy enemy tanks at a range of up to 3 kilometres. The 55-tonne Tiger I was slower than the Panther, and proved most effective in ambushes. The 69-tonne Tiger II was protected by armour up to 180 millimetres thick. One tank commander reported that a Tiger II could take twenty hits without being knocked out.

Japanese tanks

There was little scope for tank warfare in the dense jungles of south-east Asia, where World War Two was also being fought. Japan built only a small number of tanks. Their armour was so thin that American anti-tank shells, which were designed to penetrate much thicker armour, often went right through the tank before exploding.

The versatile tank

The British army used several special-purpose tanks known as 'funnies'. Among them were the flail tank, which exploded mines; the flame-thrower tank, which could project a blast of burning fuel 100 metres; and the bridge-laying and track-laying tanks. For the 1944 invasion of Normandy, the Americans produced an amphibious Sherman tank that floated ashore in an inflatable canvas boat with propellers driven by the tank's engine.

The American Sherman, seen here on the road to Italy in 1944, was the Allies' main battle tank on the Western Front. It was outclassed by the prodigious German Tigers, but so few Tigers were built – only 2000 compared to 30,000 Shermans – that they were overwhelmed by sheer force of numbers.

Fighter planes

A modern air force

The German air force – the Luftwaffe – had officially existed only since 1935. Building the Luftwaffe almost from scratch proved to be an advantage. While many air forces still relied on biplanes (double-winged planes) with bodies partly covered in fabric, the Luftwaffe was equipped with all-metal monoplanes (single-winged planes). In 1937, Germany took the world air speed record with a plane that achieved more than 600 kilometres (370 miles) per hour. This was an early Messerschmitt 109, the fighter which Hitler thought would win control of British skies.

In 1940, Hitler started preparation for an invasion of Britain. For the invasion to succeed, Britain's Royal Air Force (RAF) would have to be destroyed so that it could not protect the British Isles from invasion. The Germans hoped to achieve this with the use of bomber aeroplanes.

Bombers were heavy and slow and needed to be escorted by fighter aircraft. Fighters were lighter and could move fast and turn quickly to fire their guns at approaching enemy planes. A form of combat, known as 'dogfights', had developed between fighter planes during World War One and continued in World War Two. The aircraft would come terrifyingly close to each other to attack and make breathtaking twists and turns to avoid each other's gunfire.

The British fight back

In July 1940, Germany started its air attacks. The two-month onslaught on Britain became known as the Battle of Britain. German bombers

*The two principal fighter planes of the Battle of Britain were the Hawker Hurricane (top) and the Messerschmitt 109 (bottom). The British Hurricane was slower than the German Messerschmitt, but it was more **manoeuvrable**.*

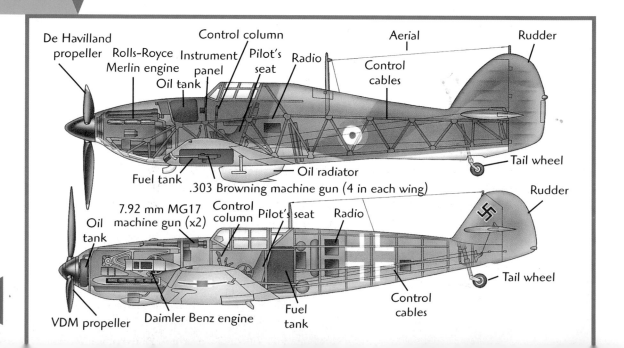

De Havilland propeller · Rolls-Royce Merlin engine · Oil tank · Control column · Instrument panel · Pilot's seat · Radio · Aerial · Control cables · Rudder · Tail wheel · Fuel tank · Oil radiator · .303 Browning machine gun (4 in each wing)

Oil tank · 7.92 mm MG17 machine gun (x2) · Control column · Pilot's seat · Radio · Rudder · Tail wheel · Control cables · Fuel tank · Daimler Benz engine · VDM propeller attacked ships and airfields and, at the beginning of September, began to bomb British cities.

The mainstay of the RAF's fighter wing was the Hawker Hurricane. Adapted from a biplane design, the Hurricane was so sturdy that it could survive damage that would have destroyed most other fighters. Although Hurricanes were credited with 80 per cent of all planes destroyed in the Battle of Britain, they were overshadowed by a new fighter plane, the Supermarine Spitfire. The Messerschmitt 109 was faster and its weapons more powerful, but the Spitfire's tight turns and better handling gave it the edge.

In a huge battle on 15 September, the RAF used all its fighter planes against the massed Luftwaffe forces. The Germans lost 60 aircraft, and two days later Hitler postponed the invasion indefinitely.

Other notable fighters

There were other fighters that were significant to the course of the war. In 1941, the Luftwaffe got the Focke-Wulf 190, another high-speed combat plane. And at the beginning of the war in the Pacific, American fighter pilots were startled to find that their Grumman Wildcats were outclassed by Japan's Mitsubishi Zero.

From 1943 many Allied fighters, such as the Hawker Typhoon, were armed with bombs and **rockets** and used to attack ground targets. The De Havilland Mosquito was one of the most versatile planes of the war. Built of plywood and powered by twin engines, it saw service as a bomber, target-finder, **reconnaissance** plane and night-fighter.

The greatest American contribution to fighter planes in Europe was the P-51 Mustang, seen here behind a group of pilots in Italy in 1944. The Mustang was as fast as the German Focke-Wulf 190, and its 1500-km (900-m) range enabled it to escort American bombers into the heart of Germany.

The first jet

In 1944, when **piston engine technology** had been pushed to its limits, the Luftwaffe introduced the Messerschmitt 262, the first jet aeroplane to see operational service. In a jet engine, the thrust comes from a high-speed stream of hot gases produced by igniting fuel mixed with compressed air. With a top speed of 864 kph (537 mph), the Messerschmitt 262 was in a league of its own. But, by this stage of the war, the Germans had hardly enough fuel to keep their fighters airborne.

Bombers

During the German invasions of Poland and France, Stuka **dive-bombers** proved to be an effective weapon against **infantry**. From September 1940 to May 1941, the Germans also used bombers to mount a campaign, called the Blitz, on London. They also bombed other British cities. But these planes carried a fairly light bomb load and the Germans never developed heavy bombers.

Mass bombing

It was the British and Americans who adopted the controversial **strategy** of mass bombing with heavy bombers. Air-Marshal 'Bomber' Harris, head of the RAF's Bomber Command, thought that huge, prolonged aerial assaults could destroy Germany's war industry. This would mean attacking targets such as weapons factories, railway centres, and fuel depots.

The city of London spreads out below a German Heinkel 111 bomber. The plane was on a raid during the Battle of Britain in 1940.

The RAF began its campaign in 1942, when it first flew the Avro Lancaster, a four-engine plane that could carry a bomb load of over 5500 kilograms. Heavy bombers sometimes flew in formations of as many as 1000 aircraft. To reduce the threat from German anti-aircraft defences, the bombers attacked at night. In the dark, however, harassed by fighters and assaulted by **flak**, many bombers missed their intended targets and simply dropped their bombs on any available built-up area.

To improve accuracy, hand-picked RAF crews, known as Pathfinder squadrons, were equipped with advanced navigation systems. Their job was to find the target and mark it with **incendiary bombs** and flares for the main bomber force. Even with the targets marked, the bombs dropped by successive waves of planes tended to creep outside the marked zone. The RAF began to call their strategy 'area bombing'. This term showed there was no distinction being made between industrial and **civilian** targets.

Daylight bombing

The Americans were convinced that precision bombing was possible only in daylight. Their B-24 Liberators and B-17 Flying Fortresses, armed with up to thirteen machine guns, were fitted with Norden bombsights. This device, in theory, enabled the Americans to hit a 30-metre circle from an altitude of 6500 metres. But the bombers proved to be neither as well-protected nor as accurate as had been hoped. During one daylight raid to Germany in August 1943, 60 out of 315 bombers were shot down. It wasn't until long-range P-51 Mustang fighters entered service as escorts for bombers in late 1943 that losses fell to an acceptable level. Even then, fewer than one third of the bombs dropped fell within 300 metres of the specific target.

Bombing from the air was not confined to Europe. On 10 March 1945, American bombers dropped 2000 tonnes of bombs on Tokyo. The resulting **firestorm** destroyed 40 per cent of the city, caused more than 125,000 **casualties** and left over a million people homeless.

Was it worth it?

The Allied bombing campaign diverted about a million German workers into reconstruction work. However, it did not cripple the German war economy until the very end, nor did it destroy civilian morale. The bombing campaign killed more than half a million German civilians. It also took a heavy toll of the attackers. More than 100,000 Allied bomber air crew lost their lives over Germany, the highest casualty rate of any branch of the Western Allies' armed forces.

The bouncing bomb

On the night of 16 May 1943, nineteen Lancaster bombers took off on a raid against three dams that supplied vital hydroelectric power and water to factories in Germany's industrial heartland. The planes carried a special type of 'bouncing bomb' invented by British scientist Barnes Wallis. Released from a height of only 27 metres, the bomb was designed to skip over the water and then slide down the face of the dam before exploding. Two of the dams were damaged, causing floods and subsequent water shortages that affected German industrial production for several months.

The kamikaze was a volunteer corps of suicide bombers in Japan. Their name means 'divine wind', and they were named after a wind that wrecked an invading fleet in the 13th century. The pilots crashed their bomb-laden planes into American ships. Despite their courage, the 1228 pilots who died on their kamikaze missions sank only 34 ships.

Airborne troops

Parachutes were first used as life-saving devices by aircrew forced to abandon their aircraft in mid-air. The parachute slows descent, so that a person hits the ground with a force no greater than if he or she had jumped off a 3-metre wall.

Surprise attacks

The Soviets were the first to realize that airborne troops equipped with parachutes – called paratroops – could be used to mount sudden attacks on targets behind enemy lines. In 1936, the Soviet army defeated an Afghan force by dropping more than 1000 paratroops in a surprise attack. The idea of soldiers attacking from planes also made a deep impression on Hitler. He described a war of the future as 'a sky black with bombers and, leaping from them into the smoke, parachute storm troops, each grasping a machine gun'.

German parachutists land in Crete in 1941. The white parachutes in the middle are those of the paratroop leaders. Although the Germans eventually captured Crete, 6000 of the invaders were killed or wounded.

As well as parachuting from planes, German airborne troops pioneered the tactic of landing in **gliders** that were towed behind planes and then released several kilometres from the target. Because the gliders were silent, they could sometimes achieve a degree of surprise denied to parachutists arriving from noisy aeroplanes. They could also deliver weapons and vehicles that were too heavy to be dropped by parachute.

First strikes from the sky

During the 1940 *blitzkrieg*, German glider troops captured the supposedly impregnable Belgian fort of Eben Emael. The next year, German airborne troops led the invasion of Crete. But here they met serious problems. Unlike modern parachutes, which can be steered, the parachutes used in World War Two left their user at the mercy of the wind. Hundreds of German paratroops landed in the sea or got tangled

Daring rescue

In 1943 the Italian dictator Benito Mussolini was toppled from power and imprisoned in a mountaintop hotel. Adolf Hitler ordered a force of glider-borne paratroops and **commandos** to rescue his ally. The gliders crash-landed in the hotel grounds, and within minutes Mussolini was bundled into a light plane and carried to freedom. He remained in hiding until 1945, when he was found and executed by communist partisans, or supporters.

in trees. The gliders could not be steered precisely, and many of them flipped over when they made forced landings. After this, Germany made no more large-scale airborne assaults.

The Allies, too, often had problems with airborne operations. When American paratroops and British glider troops spearheaded the 1943 invasion of Sicily, the parachutists ended up scattered all over south-east Sicily, and 70 of the 144 gliders crashed into the sea. It was a similar story when American paratroops were used in the invasion of the Italian mainland at Salerno. One battalion successfully reinforced the Allied invaders. Another, dropped behind German lines, was too dispersed to accomplish its mission of disrupting enemy communications.

On D-Day, 6 June 1944, when the Allies invaded France from Britain, the paratroopers were the first to arrive. Some lost their lives, landing in trees or in the cold water of the English Channel.

Failed assault

The biggest airborne assault ever was launched in September 1944 by 24,000 British and American paratroops and glider troops. Their objective was to capture key bridges in the German-occupied Netherlands. If they succeeded and held out until advancing ground troops reached them, it would open a way into Germany and might bring a quick end to the war.

British World War Two paratroopers stand by their plane before take-off. World War Two showed the hit-or-miss nature of airborne operations. Many nations continue to use airborne troops, but they rarely parachute into action.

The Americans accomplished their tasks, but the British forces landed too far from their main target at Arnhem. By the time they reached the bridge, the Germans had brought in **reinforcements**. Equipment dropped by air fell into enemy hands. After a week's fighting that cost them 7500 **casualties**, the British airborne troops surrendered.

Warships

Mighty battleships

After World War One, it appeared to some that developing air power would spell the end for battleships. Few naval leaders paid attention. Battleships were regarded as almost indestructible, and for naval powers like Britain, Japan and the USA, these mighty vessels were also symbols of national pride.

Weighing more than 35,000 tonnes, battleships were up to 300 metres long and protected by armour as much as 40 centimetres thick. They carried eight or more main guns mounted in **turrets** on the deck. Many of these guns were capable of firing a **shell** weighing about a tonne more than 30 kilometres (19 miles). Battleships also carried dozens of smaller guns, including anti-aircraft guns. Their fuel tanks held over 5000 tonnes of fuel that enabled them to cruise for thousands of kilometres. More than 1000 men were needed to crew one of these ships.

After World War One, Germany had been forbidden to build any warship over about 10,000 tonnes in weight. So the Germans built vessels known as 'pocket battleships', which were, in fact, slightly over the weight limit. The pocket battleships were armed and **armour-plated** like battleships, but were smaller in size. They had advantages, however: they were faster than more heavily-armed real battleships and better armed than smaller, faster warships.

Two damaged battleships burn in Pearl Harbor after the Japanese attack that brought the USA into World War Two.

The Bismarck and the Tirpitz

Allied battleships were positioned in the Atlantic along the routes taken by **convoys** of merchant ships bringing supplies from North America to Britain. Convoys were groups of up to 50 ships travelling together for safety and protected by armed escort ships. The main job of the battleships was to patrol in search of enemy vessels.

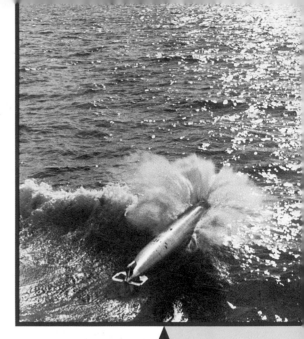

Hitler, who knew that German surface ships were no match for British naval power, ordered the construction of two 42,000-tonne battleships, the *Bismarck* and the *Tirpitz*. Their task was to destroy the Atlantic convoys. The *Bismarck* made only one combat voyage. In May 1941, after it blew up a British battlecruiser, the *Bismarck* was sunk by the Allies. The *Tirpitz* never even fought an engagement against warships. In November 1944, the ship was sunk by RAF bombers.

Battleships in the Pacific

The USA entered World War Two on 8 December 1941, the day after Japanese planes attacked their ships and planes at Pearl Harbor, Hawaii. For the rest of the Pacific war, the USA used its battleships mainly to support **infantry** landings and to protect its aircraft carriers.

Torpedoes were a type of missile used by ships and by submarines. Launched through water with the power of compressed air, they could travel several thousand metres to explode against a ship's hull.

Other warships

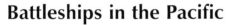

World War Two warships were designed to fight as a unit, fleet against fleet, with each type of vessel playing a different role. As it turned out, there were few fleet engagements and warships usually operated in small groups or alone.

In order of descending size, cruisers were heavily armed warships that patrolled the oceans at high speed. Destroyers were general-purpose ships, often used to protect larger ships. They were armed with torpedoes as well as guns. Lightly-armed frigates were designed mainly for **reconnaissance**. Both destroyers and frigates were extensively used as convoy escorts.

The Canadians and the British introduced the corvette, a vessel equipped mainly with anti-submarine weapons. Large numbers of minesweepers were deployed to clear the sea lanes of explosive mines. Among other fighting ships were small, very fast patrol boats armed with torpedoes.

Aircraft carriers

In the Pacific, it was not battleships but aircraft carriers that won the war at sea. By the 1930s, aircraft carriers had developed into high-speed floating air bases armed with up to 100 **dive-bombers**, torpedo planes and fighters that could attack targets 800 kilometres (500 miles) away. They heralded a new kind of warfare, in which fleets battled it out without ever coming in sight of each other.

The flight deck of a World War Two aircraft carrier as an aeroplane prepares for take-off.

Anatomy of an aircraft carrier

Americans called carriers 'flat tops' because their decks were clear of all obstacles that could interfere with planes taking off and landing. Funnels, masts and the ship's bridge were grouped to one side to maximize the flight deck area. Most of the aircraft were stowed below deck and raised on lifts as required. Carriers were armed with mainly anti-aircraft weapons for defence against attacks from the air. The guns were usually located in bays beneath the flight deck.

The flight deck – really a floating runway – was high above the water so that planes could operate in stormy seas. The largest carriers were 300 metres long, and so their flight decks were much shorter than a land runway. The aircraft were designed to take off and land at lower speeds and in shorter distances than on shore. During take-off and landing, the carrier sailed full speed into the wind, increasing lift on the aircraft's wings. Planes were also launched with steam-powered catapults that could accelerate a 3-tonne aircraft to more than 100 kilometres per hour (62 miles per hour) in just 17 metres. When they landed, the planes were slowed down by wires strung across the flight deck which hooked into the underside of the aircraft.

Assault on Pearl Harbor

Japan's carrier fleet had been built up as the navy's main strike force by Admiral Isoroku Yamamoto. In their attack on the American base at Pearl Harbor, Japanese warplanes launched from six carriers destroyed or crippled eighteen American warships. The Japanese also destroyed 188 aircraft and damaged another 159. But by chance, all the Americans carriers were at sea on that day. Yamamoto knew that the failure to eliminate them could have serious consequences. 'The sinking of four or five battleships is no cause for celebration,' he wrote.

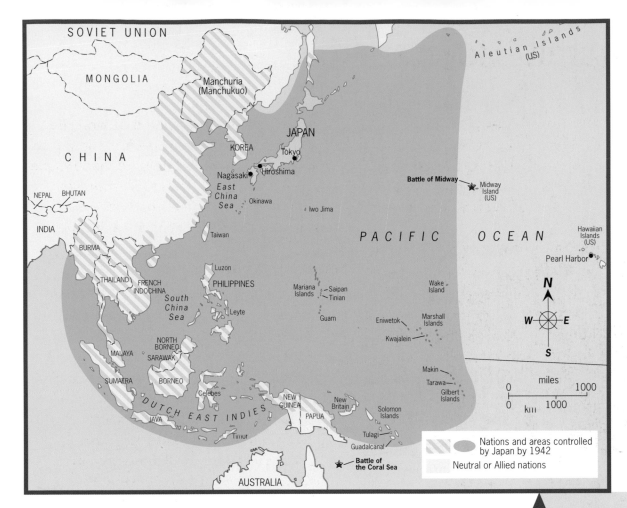

The map legend:

Battle of Midway ★ Midway Island (US)

Battle of the Coral Sea ★

Nations and areas controlled by Japan by 1942

Neutral or Allied nations

Battles in the Pacific Ocean

The first engagement between carrier fleets came in May 1942, in the Coral Sea north of Australia. One American carrier was sunk and another badly damaged, while one Japanese carrier was destroyed and two damaged. The Americans repaired their damaged carrier within 72 hours, but the Japanese ships remained out of action for months.

By then, Japan had already lost the vital battle for control of the Pacific. Yamamoto knew that Japan could not win a long war against the USA, and planned a bold move to destroy what remained of the American fleet in the Pacific. He would invade Midway, an American-occupied island, and then attack the US fleet when it steamed to the rescue.

What Yamamoto did not know was that the Americans had discovered his intentions by breaking Japan's secret codes. And he mistakenly thought that both US carriers had been sunk in the Coral Sea. On the morning of 4 June 1942, the Japanese found themselves under attack from planes launched from carriers which they had assumed didn't exist. For the loss of one carrier and 150 planes, the Americans destroyed four Japanese carriers and 322 planes. After the Battle of Midway, American task forces gradually imposed their domination on the Pacific.

Until the Americans entered World War Two with their fleet of aircraft carriers, the Japanese had control of a large part of the Pacific islands and nations. The Battle of Midway stopped the Japanese advance and was a turning point in the war.

Amphibious warfare

High-risk operations

One of the riskiest military operations is that of landing troops on heavily-defended coastlines. When Canadian and British troops raided the French port of Dieppe in 1942, more than two-thirds of them were killed, captured or wounded.

Despite the risks involved, the USA had to mount **amphibious** assaults if they were to capture the Pacific islands that led like stepping stones to Japan. To do this they used special assault craft. While warships and aircraft attacked the Japanese defences, the **infantry** raced ashore in landing craft. Timing was critical. If the bombardment stopped too soon, the defenders could slaughter the invaders while they were still in the sea. If the bombardment went on too long, the attackers risked being killed by their own side once they were on land.

Landing craft

The Americans developed several types of landing craft, ranging from small personnel carriers to vessels that could carry tanks and bulldozers, as well as men. Most landing craft were boxy vessels with drawbridge-style bow doors that dropped flat when the craft reached shore so that the attackers could run directly onto the beach. Sometimes, however, the invaders misjudged the depth of the water and the landing craft grounded a long way from the beach, forcing the invaders to wade ashore under heavy fire. That is what happened at the island of Tarawa in 1943, where many landing craft got stuck. The 5000 Japanese defenders inflicted 3000 **casualties** before they were overcome.

The American fleet in the Pacific included cruisers, destroyers, assault craft, and transport vehicles. Many of these vessels can be seen below as troops and supplies are landed on the island of Okinawa during the Allied advance towards Japan.

The Normandy invasion

The Allies also invaded Italy and North Africa from the sea. However, these assaults were small compared to the huge Operation Neptune,

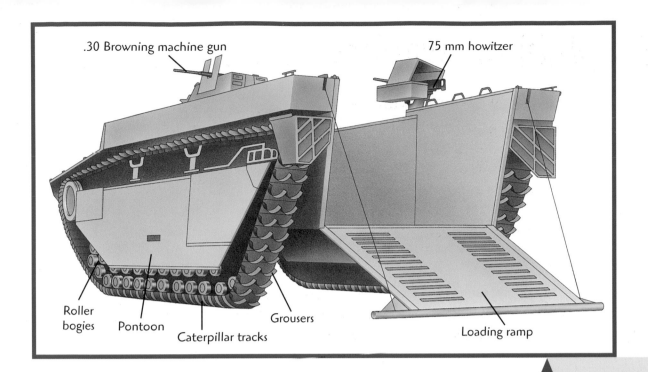

.30 Browning machine gun

75 mm howitzer

Roller bogies

Pontoon

Caterpillar tracks

Grousers

Loading ramp

the naval phase of the invasion of France on 6 June 1944. Neptune called for the landing of 170,000 men in a single day on five beaches along the Normandy coast. An armada of 4000 landing craft, supported by 1000 warships and other vessels, was assembled to put this force ashore. More than 10,000 fighters, bombers and **barrage** balloons provided protection overhead.

Artificial harbours

The Germans didn't know where the invasion would take place, but they were sure that it would be directed against a port. Therefore they concentrated their defences on established harbours. Instead, the Allies brought their own harbours with them in order to land on the beaches they had chosen. The two artificial harbours, called 'Mulberries', were mammoth feats of engineering. More than 200 steel and concrete sections, weighing up to 6000 tonnes each, were used in their construction. There were 33 jetties connected by 16 kilometres (10 miles) of floating roadway. The sections were assembled in dockyards all round Britain and towed to Normandy by 160 tugboats. The Allies also laid an undersea oil pipeline from the Isle of Wight, off the south coast of England.

On the chosen morning, called D-Day, the landing craft were launched up to 20 kilometres (12 miles) from the French coast. More than 130,000 soldiers got ashore in the first sixteen hours, and within ten days, ships were unloading supplies in the artificial harbours. By the end of June, the Allies had landed 850,000 men and 150,000 vehicles on French soil.

After their disastrous landing at Tarawa, the Americans used many more amphibious tractors, known as 'amtracks'. Amtracks had propellers to drive them through the water and **caterpillar tracks** *to carry them over reefs and up onto beaches.*

Submarines

Cutting off supplies

By the summer of 1940, when much of Europe had fallen to the Nazis, Britain was still holding out against Germany. The island nation depended for its survival on supplies shipped from overseas. If this lifeline could be cut, Britain would be forced to surrender. In a series of attacks known as the Battle of the Atlantic, Germany tried to starve Britain into submission by attacking merchant ships from beneath the waves.

Germany's main weapon was a submarine. The Type VII U-boat was driven by diesel engines on the surface and by a battery-powered motor under water. U-boats lay in wait along the routes taken by **convoys**. They could detect targets by picking up the sound of propellers with an underwater microphone called a hydrophone. The U-boats usually approached under the surface, using a **periscope** to keep the ship in view. Once the target was in range, the U-boat fired at it with torpedoes. If there were warships nearby, the U-boat then dived deeper to make its escape. A U-boat could descend to 200 metres and stay submerged for many hours before surfacing for air and to recharge its batteries.

Heavy losses

To maximize their effectiveness, U-boats were organized into groups known as 'wolf-packs'. When a U-boat captain sighted a convoy, he would communicate its position and shadow it until the rest of the pack closed in for the kill. U-boats inflicted heavy losses on convoys in the Atlantic: in one attack on a convoy in 1942, a wolf pack sank 22 out of 103 ships.

The hunters become the hunted

The attacks continued successfully into the spring of 1943. Then, Allied shipping losses suddenly dropped while U-boat losses mounted sharply. There were several reasons for this reversal. More convoy escort ships were built and fitted with new detection systems. The development of longer-range aircraft meant the Allies could patrol further out into the

A surfaced U-boat under attack by Allied aircraft during the Battle of the Atlantic.

Atlantic. And British code-breakers had broken the U-boat radio communications code. By reading enemy messages, the Allies could route convoys out of harm's way and hunt down U-boats that had given away their positions. Germany had, briefly, come close to defeating Britain with its U-boats, but at a heavy cost: 28,000 of the 40,000 men who served in U-boats were killed.

The American submarine force

After the Japanese attack on Pearl Harbor, the US Navy entered World War Two in 1941 with only 14 working submarines in the Pacific. During the war, another 130 arrived from American shipyards. The USA used these in long-range attacks in Japanese-controlled Pacific waters.

Anti-submarine weapons and submarine tracking devices

Depth-charges were underwater bombs. Explosive-packed steel drums, they were set to go off at a certain depth when dropped near their targets.

Hedgehogs fired small bombs from warships, such as destroyers or corvettes. The bombs were fired ahead of the vessels. This was a more effective way of attacking a submarine than with depth-charges, which were discharged after the ship had passed over a U-boat. Unlike depth-charges, the bombs exploded only on contact with a U-boat.

Asdic (an early form of **sonar**) stood for Anti-Submarine Detection Investigation Committee. It sent out sound waves to detect and locate submarines. If the sound waves struck a U-boat, they were reflected to a receiver and transmitted as a loud 'ping'. This is called echolocation.

Huff-duff (high-frequency direction finder) tuned in to U-boat radio transmissions. When two or more Huff-duff stations picked up a U-boat signal, the submarine's approximate position could be plotted.

Microwave radar was a type of **radar** (radio detection and ranging) operating on very short wavelengths. Unlike long-wave radar, microwave radar signals could not be detected by U-boats.

A view of a sinking Japanese ship from the periscope of an American submarine. The United States' submarines accounted for two-thirds of Japan's merchant shipping losses and about one-third of its naval losses. They sank one battleship, eleven cruisers and eight aircraft carriers, including the 71,000-tonne Shinano, the largest vessel to be sunk in the war.

Radar

A new detection device

Before World War Two, people believed that 'the bomber will always get through'. That they didn't is largely due to **radar**, a system for detecting and locating objects. Developed in the 1930s, radar works by bouncing a radio beam off a metallic object such as an aircraft or ship. By measuring the time taken for the echo to reach a receiver, the radar operator can estimate the range and course of the plane or ship. Radar also enables pilots to navigate at night. Although radar served all of the armed forces, it was the air war that accelerated its development.

The British advantage

Britain quickly recognized the importance of radar. When the Battle of Britain began, the RAF had a chain of radar stations that could detect enemy aeroplanes and direct Allied fighters to engage them. With this early-warning system, RAF interceptors could take off at the last possible minute and therefore their fuel supplies would outlast those of the German fighters. The Germans underestimated the value of the British radar system and made no systematic effort to destroy it.

The British secretly developed a miniature airborne radar set. In November 1940, a radar-equipped Bristol Beaufighter shot down a German bomber at night. To explain the success without giving away the radar secret, the RAF claimed that its night-fighter crews were selected from pilots with exceptional eyesight who were fed on a diet rich in carrots (which were said to improve vision).

Countermeasures

By the time the Allies began their mass bombing campaign, Germany had set up its own radar stations. The Germans had one radar plotting an incoming bomber's course and another directing a night-fighter towards the attacker. The British learned how to **jam** the signals to the German stations, but Germany quickly fitted its night-fighters with radar sets that enabled them to find targets without any input from the ground.

Devious devices

The British developed many countermeasures against German air defences. MANDREL was a jamming device against the German early-warning radar system. TINSEL **amplified** the sound of a bomber's engines to drown out the German fighters' radio communications. BOOZER was a set carried in the bomber to warn the pilot when he had been detected by enemy radar.

Cat and mouse over Germany

In late 1942, the RAF introduced a remote navigation system code-named OBOE, which used two radar stations about 160 kilometres (100 miles) apart. One station, called 'cat', directed a bomber by radar pulses. The other station, called 'mouse', signalled the aircraft to drop its bombs when it reached its target. But OBOE's range was limited and it could direct only one aircraft at a time. Early in 1943, a better system was found. British and American bombers were equipped with H2S, a radar set that could 'map' the ground even under cloud and pick out targets up to 40 kilometres (25 miles) ahead.

The Germans then developed airborne radar sets which enabled their fighters to home in on H2S signals. But the British countered once again with WINDOW, a method of confusing enemy radar systems by dropping aluminium strips that reflected radar beams. This technique was first used in raids on Hamburg, Germany, in the summer of 1943. As the RAF planes made their bombing runs, the crews heaved bundles of WINDOW strips out of the aircraft. On the German radar screens, the blips of the bombers were lost in what appeared to be a heavy snowstorm.

*Radar was used not just in the air, but for sea operations, too. In this operations room in the dungeons of Dover Castle on the British coast, radar information was gathered and used to direct coastal **artillery** in attacks on enemy ships.*

Communications

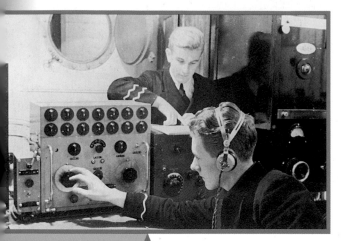

Radio operators on a French ship listen out for signals of distress from other ships.

New developments in radio **technology** transformed communications on the World War Two battlefield. Radios did not require cables, as field telephones and the **telegraph** had done in World War One. Instead, radio messages and signals were transmitted through the air without the use of wires. By bouncing signals off a layer of the atmosphere called the ionosphere, messages were transmitted over the airwaves hundreds or even thousands of kilometres. Radio communication was vital to all branches of the armed forces, but its greatest impact was felt by the ground forces. In World War One, army commanders had often been left helpless spectators of the battles they were supposed to be directing. In World War Two, the instant communication provided by radios gave them important advantages. Commanders could now respond immediately to control troop movements, call up **reinforcements** or air support, and direct **artillery** fire.

Leading from the front

Radio was not new, but radio sets had become more portable since World War One. Compact **electronic** devices called **vacuum tubes** were used to **amplify** radio signals, making it possible to build radio sets small enough to be carried by a single man.

Some generals took advantage of the new **technology** to command battles from close to the **front line**, rather than from headquarters in the rear. General Hans Guderian, Germany's leading *blitzkrieg* commander, who had served as a signals officer in World War One, kept up with his troops in a radio-equipped command vehicle. The American general, George Patton, used radio to lead from the front. Patton said that armies were like a piece of spaghetti: you couldn't push a piece of spaghetti, you had to pull it. The British commander Bernard Montgomery used radio broadcasts to boost the morale of his troops. He became the first general in history to broadcast directly to his forces.

All German tanks were equipped with radio, which enabled them to co-ordinate their movements. Panzer tanks often defeated larger Soviet armoured forces because of this advantage. Only the Soviet commanders' vehicles were fitted with radio and instructions to the rest of the tank unit were passed on by crewmen waving signal flags. German tank crews could recognize the Soviet command vehicle by its aerial and always tried to destroy it first. If the command vehicle was knocked out, the rest of the unit, lacking clear instructions about what to do next, often became confused and demoralized.

Clear signal

The German army, however, used low-frequency AM (amplitude modulation) radio, which suffers from atmospheric interference and can easily be **jammed**. The Americans used high-frequency FM (frequency modulation) radio, an American invention of the 1930s. FM eliminated interference to produce a signal much clearer than AM, and was difficult to jam. The value that the US forces attached to communications was shown in the strength of their Signal Corps, the men and women who installed, operated and maintained the communications equipment. It grew from 27,000 at the war's outset to about 350,000 by war's end.

The USA had the best communications equipment in World War Two. This American mortar crew could remain in constant touch with its commander or headquarters through its portable radio.

Soldiers used radio to get news from the outside world as well as for communication. These Germans, cut off in their underground living quarters, tune in to a radio broadcast.

The code-breakers

During World War Two, radio transmissions were often intercepted by the enemy. Because of this, important radio messages were sent in codes, or secret symbols or words. Each side in the war eavesdropped on the other and used **cryptanalysts** to try and crack the secrets of their enemies' codes.

Enigma

The Germans invented what they thought was an unbreakable secret code based on an encoding machine called Enigma. (Enigma means 'mystery'.) The machine resembled a typewriter, with a keyboard and a panel of individually lettered lamps. When the operator pressed a key, one of the letters lit up. The process also worked in reverse, so that if pressing key B produced the letter K, pressing key K produced the letter B. This produced a message that was unreadable unless the person at the other end also had an Enigma machine.

The Enigma message was then transmitted by radio in Morse code. (This international code sends messages using a pattern of short and long noises or flashes to represent letters of the alphabet.) A radio operator receiving an Enigma message in Morse turned it into letters and then typed it out on another Enigma machine to produce the original message. The Enigma machine had billions of possible settings, which were changed daily so that the enemy would never get a chance to catch up and break the code. The weakness of the system was that the sender had to let the receiver know which setting to use.

British cryptanalysts used a kind of **electromechanical** computer called a Bombe to find settings that would turn

These German signal troops are using an Enigma machine, although the official description at the time was a 'teletype'. The Allies managed to keep their seizure of an Enigma machine a secret, and the Germans went on using Enigma codes until the end of the war.

an Enigma message into plain German. Their job was made much easier after May 1941, when a British destroyer seized an Enigma machine and a list of settings from a crippled U-boat. Within a week, the cryptanalysts had cracked the German U-boat code. There were occasional setbacks when the Germans upgraded their Enigma machines, but the Allied code-breakers could often read U-boat signals within hours of their interception.

A code-cracking computer

The Germans used another code, called Fish, which was even more complex than the Enigma codes. To crack it, British scientists developed the first **electronic** computer, Colossus, which could test messages at the rate of 5000 characters a second. It helped decipher German messages showing that Hitler believed the Allied invasion of France would take place near Calais rather than in Normandy.

Japan's open secrets

The Japanese also developed a navy code that they believed was unbreakable. In fact, the Americans cracked it within four months. It was thanks to the code-breakers that US forces uncovered Admiral Yamamoto's plan for the attack on Midway Island. In April 1943, American code-breakers decrypted a message revealing that Admiral Yamamoto would be flying to the island of Bougainville. When the admiral arrived, a force of P-38 fighters intercepted his plane and shot it out of the sky.

The ability to read Japanese naval codes meant that the Americans knew the whereabouts of Japan's warships for most of the Pacific war. Their lack of secure codes probably cost Japan a third of their shipping fleet.

Before the invention of computers made the task easier, de-coding enemy messages in World War Two was done by people on manual decoders such as this one. It was a laborious process of trial and error. A computer did the same thing but thousands of times faster.

Navajo code

The US Marine Corps in the Pacific used a simple, but effective, voice code. Navajo Native Americans serving with the Marines transmitted messages in their complex, unwritten language. This was understood by only a handful of non-Navajos. The Japanese never succeeded in breaking this minority language 'code'.

The propaganda weapon

UNITED
we are strong

UNITED we will win

Warring nations have always used propaganda to raise the morale of their citizens and dishearten their enemies. In World War Two, radio and film **technology** offered increased opportunities for manipulating the attitudes of **civilians**. Propaganda was aimed at civilians both at home and abroad. On both sides, radio broadcasts were made to enemy nations with the aim of undermining loyalty, changing opinions and sowing seeds of doubt. On the other hand, cinema audiences flocked to films glorifying the efforts of brave men and women in their armed forces.

Everywhere, posters exhorted citizens to do their bit, maintain security and support their country's efforts. Aircraft made it possible to distribute printed propaganda in enemy territory as well. For the first few months of the war, British bombers dropped millions of propaganda leaflets on Germany.

Propaganda was often direct and simple, designed to inspire loyalty and build support for the war effort. This poster encourages civilians to trust that the united efforts and weapons of the Allies would win the war.

Radio propaganda

As the Nazi Minister for Public Enlightenment and Propaganda, Josef Goebbels was in complete control of the German press and radio. He encouraged German citizens to buy cheap, mass-produced radio sets that could only receive German stations. When war broke out, 70 per cent of German households had radios, the highest percentage in the world. Compulsory listening was introduced, and loudspeakers were installed in factories. Listening to any non-German controlled station was a crime punishable by death.

In nations where the media was not under complete state control, there was still censorship (banning of certain information) in wartime. British and American radio stations censored programmes which they thought might breach security or damage morale. They tended to exaggerate victories and play down defeats, but in general told the truth.

British Prime Minister Winston Churchill and US President Franklin D Roosevelt used radio to speak directly to the people. Churchill stirred his listeners with rousing speeches that did not flinch from giving bad news. Roosevelt adopted a reassuring tone in his regular 'fireside chats'. By contrast, Hitler rarely addressed the German public after 1942. Goebbels was forced to build up a picture of the Nazi leader as a man working night and day to save Germany.

Germany's minister of propaganda Josef Goebbels makes a radio broadcast during World War Two. Goebbels believed that radio was the most important means of influencing the population.

Propaganda of death

The Nazis whipped up hatred against Jews so that few people would object when the government stripped the Jews of their property and legal rights. Goebbels came up with slogans such as, 'The Jews are our misfortune.' Julius Streicher, a publisher who was executed after the war for his 'propaganda of death', filled the pages of his newspaper with obscene caricatures of Jews.

Hitler used the cover of war to carry out his 'final solution'. This meant the murder of all Jews in German-occupied territories. In a kind of reverse propaganda, any mention of this **genocide** was forbidden. Although there were rumours, the terrible truth was not uncovered until the war ended.

Japanese propaganda

The Japanese propaganda effort was aimed at persuading the people of south-east Asia that Japan was liberating them from colonial powers. At home, the Japanese were kept in ignorance of the course of the war. Defeats were hushed up. After the Battle of Midway, the wounded Japanese sailors were brought ashore at night in secret and treated in isolation wards. Even Japanese politicians were not told of the disaster.

Famous propagandists

Radio propaganda was used to lower enemy morale. One famous figure, Tokyo Rose (actually an American named Iva Togori D'Aquino) broadcast a daily programme from Japan heard by American servicemen in the Pacific. She was later arrested for treason. Lord Haw-Haw, who broadcast throughout the war from Germany to the UK, was also an American, William Joyce. He had lived in England for much of his life and was a fascist. In his radio programme, Joyce spouted Nazi propaganda in an upper-class British accent. After the war, Joyce was hanged for treason.

The home front

Right from the start, the Allies committed all their human and industrial resources to the war effort. Factories switched from the production of peacetime products, such as cars, to wartime necessities, such as aircraft and ships. They operated around the clock, and women were drafted into the workforce.

On the US **home front**, aircraft production rose from below 6000 in 1941 to more than 96,000 in 1945 thanks to the improved techniques and the influx of women workers. Shipbuilding also boomed. Using mass-production methods, the United States launched 140 freighters a month in 1943. These vessels, called Liberty ships, were constructed to a standardized design with prefabricated sections. One Liberty ship was built in only 80 hours, 30 minutes. The USA was able to supply not only its own military needs, but also provided more than one-quarter of Britain's and the Soviet Union's.

Germany's folly

Compared to the combined industrial muscle of the Allies, the Nazis were slow to introduce an all-out war effort. Until 1941, Germany's factories operated much as they had in peacetime. Production of ordinary domestic products actually rose. Hitler had promised a quick victory and was reluctant to admit that the war might drag on for years. He refused to allow women to join the labour force. Their job, said his propaganda chief Josef Goebbels, was 'being beautiful and having children'.

A trainee welder works on the construction of a Liberty ship. Six million women workers helped double industrial output in the United States during World War Two.

> *War is won in the factories.*
>
> Soviet leader Josef Stalin.

Forced labour

As the war continued, Nazi Germany tried to solve its manpower problem by using Jews and other prisoners of war as forced labour. Many of these workers were fed on starvation rations, housed in appalling conditions and denied medical care. The Nazis tried to justify this treatment by claiming that Jews and Soviets were sub-human. But in 1943, the Soviet Union – where women made up more than half the labour force – produced twice as many armoured fighting vehicles as Germany did.

Japan's ruin

Japan didn't have the raw materials to fight a long war. All of its oil and most of its steel had to be imported. The nation had survived at the beginning of the war by plundering the nations it had conquered in the Pacific. But once the Allies won control of the Pacific Ocean, Japan was doomed.

A US poster encourages **civilians** to save scrap metal that can be recycled to make weapons and **ammunition**.

A factory produces synthetic rubber gas masks used to protect soldiers and civilians against poisonous gas attacks.

Synthetic rubber and fuel

In 1939, the USA used half of all the world's natural rubber. Ninety per cent of the rubber came from countries that were occupied by the Japanese. When supplies dried up, the Americans launched a crash programme to develop a synthetic substitute. By 1945, the United States was producing nearly a million tonnes of synthetic rubber a year.

Germany had to import most of its fuel oil. When supplies were cut off by the advancing Soviet army, the Germans began producing synthetic fuel from coal. In 1945, 85 per cent of the fuel used by German aircraft was synthetic, but there simply wasn't enough to keep the planes flying.

Rockets and guided missiles

Hitler's wonder weapons

In the summer of 1944, as the Allies closed in on Germany, Hitler launched his 'wonder weapons', the V–1 and V–2. (The V stood for *vergeltung* or 'reprisal'.) The V–1 (dubbed the 'buzz bomb' or 'doodlebug' by Londoners) was really a jet-propelled pilotless aircraft, rather than a **rocket**. It carried an 850-kilogram **warhead** and had a range of about 250 kilometres (155 miles). The V–1's course was preset and regulated by an autopilot, a magnetic compass and a propeller-driven distance counter. When the set distance was reached, the engine's fuel supply cut off and the V–1 plunged to the ground. Once the engine stopped, people on the ground knew they had only about fifteen seconds to reach shelter.

Fighting the V-1 menace

More than 10,000 V–1s were launched by the Germans against Britain before the Allies overran their launch sites in France. Altogether, nearly 2500 V–1s hit London. They killed more than 6000 people, injured 17,000 and damaged about 23,000 homes. Although they were not particularly reliable or accurate, V–1s were cheaper to make than aeroplanes and did more damage than German bombers had in the Battle of Britain.

The flying bombs were fairly slow and flew on fixed courses at low altitudes. Because of this, they could be intercepted by fighters, including Britain's first jet, the Gloster Meteor. Since there was a risk of fighters blowing themselves up if they **detonated** the warheads at too close a range, pilots learned how to nudge the V–1s onto courses that would make them crash harmlessly in thinly populated areas.

Allied anti-aircraft guns had little success against the V–1s until they began using a **radar**-guided

Allied airmen examine parts of a V–2 rocket that fell in Belgium. About 3000 V–2s were fired by the Germans in World War Two.

system. This was coupled with an **electronic** aiming device which automatically adjusted itself to the V–1's course and speed – it could aim a **shell** at a position in the sky where the V–1 would be when the shell arrived. Radio-controlled **fuses** then detonated the shells when they came within range of their target. The combination of these three devices worked so well that in the last major V–1 attack, only four of the ninety-four missiles launched got through.

The V–2

There was no defence against the V–2, a liquid-fuelled rocket which rose 80 kilometres (50 miles) into the sky and descended at 5000 kilometres per hour (3100 miles per hour). It exploded before its victims heard its sonic boom.

After Germany surrendered, both the USA and the Soviet Union used V–2 scientists to develop their own rocket programmes. Wernher von Braun, seen here at an American rocket launch, oversaw the development of intercontinental ballistic missiles and the rockets that would take American astronauts to the Moon in 1969.

The V–2 was designed by rocket engineer Wernher von Braun and was Germany's biggest weapons project. Its production employed 20,000 people, mainly slave labourers. The problem with the V–2 was its expense. It cost 50 times as much to make as a V–1, yet carried a warhead that was only slightly bigger.

If Germany had developed its V weapons a few months earlier, it is possible that they might have delayed the Allied invasion of France. In the event, the weapons came too late to affect the course of the war. But their deadly potential was not lost on military strategists and scientists. The V–1 was one of the first long-range, **guided missiles**. The unstoppable V–2, with its high **trajectory** and **supersonic** descent, was an early **ballistic missile**. Both represented significant steps in the development of weapons of the future.

The atomic bomb

Two days before the outbreak of World War Two, the Danish scientist Niels Bohr published an article outlining the theory of nuclear energy. If an atom of a heavy **element**, such as uranium or plutonium, is split, the energy released can produce an explosion of colossal power. When Bohr discovered that German scientists had found a method of splitting uranium, he contacted the German-born Jewish physicist Albert Einstein, who had settled in the United States when Hitler came to power. Einstein wrote to President Roosevelt, warning him that the Nazis might develop a type of nuclear weapon called an atomic bomb.

Race to build the bomb

Einstein's warning resulted in what was then the largest enterprise in the history of science. A $2 billion programme to make the first nuclear weapon crammed about thirty years of **technological** development into under five years. Code-named the Manhattan Project, the USA's race to build the bomb employed more than 40,000 people at 37 secret installations across the United States and Canada. The largest site was at Oak Ridge, Tennessee, where a plant was built to process uranium. Plutonium was produced at Hanford in the state of Washington.

The atomic bomb was tested only once, on 16 July 1945, when a piece of plutonium the size of a tennis ball exploded in the New Mexico desert with a blast equivalent to 20,000 tonnes of conventional explosives.

The actual design and building of the uranium and plutonium bombs took place at Los Alamos, New Mexico, under the direction of the American physicist J Robert Oppenheimer. Many of the scientists recruited by Oppenheimer were German-Jewish exiles driven from Germany by Hitler's anti-Jewish policies. Germany still had scientists who were capable of developing a bomb, but Hitler was not interested in doing so. He scornfully dismissed nuclear weapons as 'Jewish physics'.

The Manhattan Project therefore turned out to be a race with only one competitor. There were many hurdles. One of the biggest was how to make a 'trigger' that would make the nuclear material explode with maximum release of energy. Eventually the scientists came up with two methods. For uranium, one mass of uranium was fired at terrific **velocity** at another mass of uranium. For plutonium, the nuclear material was

packed in explosives which, when **detonated**, concentrated the plutonium so that the entire mass exploded almost instantaneously. The USA now had its nuclear weapons.

The decision to drop the bomb

By the summer of 1945, Germany had been defeated but Japan continued to fight the Allies in the Pacific. The Americans were considering an invasion of Japan, which they reckoned would cost them as many as 250,000 **casualties**.

Instead, US President Harry Truman (who had taken over on Roosevelt's death) ordered the terrible new weapon to be deployed. On 6 August 1945, a B–29 Superfortress plane dropped a uranium atomic bomb on the Japanese city of Hiroshima. It killed 80,000 **civilians** in seconds. Three days later, a plutonium atomic bomb was detonated over Japan at Nagasaki, a city of 212,000 people. The bomb immediately killed one-third of the population and injured a further 77,000. In both cities, more than twice as many victims died later, from **radiation sickness**. One week later, on 14 August 1945, Japan surrendered. World War Two was over.

A Japanese mother and son sit inside a shack where their house used to be. They built the shack out of the wreckage left after the atomic bomb was dropped on Nagasaki.

The unleashed power of the atom has changed everything save our modes of thinking and we thus drift towards unparalleled catastrophe.

Albert Einstein on the significance of the atom bomb. Einstein knew that human beings now had immense power for destruction but perhaps not the wisdom to control this power.

Medicine

There were no medical defences against the devastation of **radiation**, but generally the wounded of World War Two had a better chance of survival than in any previous conflict. The death rate among hospitalized American soldiers fell to only four per cent from fifty per cent a hundred years earlier. The reasons for this improvement were new drugs, better surgical techniques and the use of motorized ambulances and planes. In the Allied campaign that followed the invasion of France, over 100,000 **casualties** were **evacuated** by air.

A wounded US Marine on the island of Tarawa in the Pacific is given plasma to replace lost blood. The new method of separating and storing plasma saved many lives in World War Two.

Plasma

Blood **transfusions** had saved the lives of many World War One soldiers suffering from heavy blood loss. But the problem with blood is that, even when refrigerated, it deteriorates within two days. In 1938, Dr Charles Drew, an American transfusion specialist, discovered that by separating plasma (the liquid part of blood) from the blood cells and then refrigerating them separately, they could be recombined up to a week later for a transfusion.

Drew also discovered that plasma, unlike whole blood, could be given to anyone regardless of their blood type. Plasma-only transfusions were good for treating World War Two burn victims who lost a lot of fluid but few blood cells. Other researchers discovered how to increase the shelf life of plasma by freeze-drying it and sealing it in plastic bags. When it was needed for a transfusion, the dried plasma was simply mixed with sterile water.

Anti-bacterial drugs

Sulfanilamide, an **anti-bacterial** drug first used in 1936, was issued to troops in both the Allied and German armies. Every soldier carried a first aid pack containing a package of sulfa powder which was dusted onto open wounds. Sulfanilamide saved the lives of many Allied soldiers fighting in the jungles of south-east Asia, where even minor wounds quickly became infected if left untreated.

DDT

Insects transmitted a number of diseases, such as typhus, which were major killers in the conflicts before World War Two. DDT, the first synthetic chemical **insecticide**, was mass-produced from 1939. When US troops captured Naples in Italy in 1943, they discovered that typhus had broken out. They prevented an **epidemic** by dusting almost the whole population with DDT powder. The Americans also virtually eradicated malaria in Italy by spraying swampland with the chemical. DDT was called a 'saviour of mankind' when it was introduced. However, it was banned by many countries in the 1970s after scientists discovered that it built up in the food-chain, poisoning insect-eating animals and their predators.

The first antibiotic

A huge breakthrough in the treatment of infection with **antibiotics** occurred during World War Two. Penicillin had been discovered in 1928 by the Scottish bacteriologist Alexander Fleming, who obtained it from certain types of mould. Although Fleming demonstrated that penicillin had remarkable anti-bacterial properties, he could not produce it in useful quantities. When war broke out, British scientists asked American scientists to help. It took three years to find a way to mass-produce penicillin, but it was available when Allied forces launched the D-Day invasion in 1944.

Fighting malaria

In the Far East, malaria transmitted by mosquito bites killed more soldiers than bombs or bullets did. Even when malaria was not fatal, it caused a fever that made soldiers too ill to fight. Malaria hospitalized more than half of the British Commonwealth soldiers serving in Burma in 1942. By 1945 the use of anti-malarial drugs, such as **quinine,** had cut the sickness rate by more than 90 per cent. The Americans used a synthetic anti-malarial drug called Atabrine. It had unpleasant side effects, including headaches and nausea. Medics watched over servicemen at meal times, making sure that each man swallowed his dose before he was allowed to eat.

Penicillin goes into mass production. Workers on an assembly line prepare vials of the much-needed antibiotic for packing and shipping to the battlefronts.

A scientific revolution

The nature of the weapons and the advances in **technology** in World War Two helped to make it the most lethal conflict in history. Over 50 million people died during the war. More than half of these people were **civilians**.

War changes science

The most important technological developments were **radar**, the **electronic** computer, the **ballistic missile** and the atomic bomb. These were the work of teams of scientists, and their success changed the way in which science was conducted. Before the war, most scientific advances were made by individuals or small groups following their own lines of research. After World War Two, government and industry became the main employers of scientists. In a sense, World War Two was the time in which science, until then seen as a force for good, lost its innocence.

The nuclear age

The atomic bombs that exploded over Japan in 1945 cast a shadow that still hasn't lifted. In 1949 the Soviet Union tested its own atomic bomb, an action that started a nuclear weapons race with the USA. In the late 1950s, nuclear **warheads** were fitted to long-range missiles based on the design of Germany's V-2 **rocket**. These exposed everybody on the planet to the risk of nuclear attack. In the 1960s, the Americans installed nuclear missiles on submarines, the design of which owed a lot to German U-boats.

A descendant of World War Two weapons, this air defence system has a multiple launcher holding four lethal missiles. The launcher is positioned between a radar and an optical tracker system.

The threat of mutual destruction has deterred world powers from using nuclear weapons. But dozens of wars have been fought with other weapons developed or improved in World War Two. By the outbreak of the Korean War in 1950, jet fighters had largely replaced **piston engine** warplanes. In the 1991 Gulf War, the USA attacked Iraqi targets with cruise missiles, a high-technology development from Germany's V-1s. Tanks and other armoured fighting vehicles remain the main **offensive** weapons of land warfare.

Weapons systems

World War Two marked the beginning of the evolution of weapons into high-tech 'weapons systems'. A modern battle tank, for example, bristles with offensive and defensive devices. These include communications equipment, target-detecting sensors, computer-guided and **laser**-guided aiming devices, and equipment to protect the crew from attack by chemical or biological weapons.

Everyday technology

Much of the technology developed for World War Two military purposes has been adapted to peacetime use. Nuclear power has been harnessed to provide energy. The jet engine has made it possible for travellers to fly swiftly around the world. Radar technology means these journeys can be made safely even when visibility is poor, and by night as well as day. Electronic computers have become standard tools for communication and processing information. The USA's synthetic rubber programme laid the foundations of the modern plastics industry. **Antibiotics** have saved countless lives. **Insecticides** have reduced disease and boosted crop yields, although at a cost to the environment.

This B–2 plane can carry nearly 20 tonnes of nuclear or non-nuclear weapons on long-range missions. It is called a 'stealthy' aircraft because it is hard to detect by radar due to its shape and construction.

Timeline

1928	Discovery of penicillin
1931	Development of radar begins in Britain
1933	Hitler comes to power in Germany
1935	26 February: Radar successfully tested
1936	First use (by Soviet Union) of parachutes to attack behind enemy lines
	First use of sulfanimide as anti-bacterial drug
1937	Messerschmitt 109 takes world air speed record
1938	Charles Drew successfully separates blood plasma from blood cells and stores for transfusions
1939	Mass production of DDT begins
	29 August: Soviet Union signs non-aggression pact with Germany
	1 September: Germany invades Poland
	3 September: Britain and France declare war on Germany
1940	First use of German 88 mm as anti-tank weapon
	First use of airborne radar set
	10 May: Germany invades Denmark, Norway, Belgium, the Netherlands and France
	10 June: Italy declares war on France and Britain
	July–September: Battle of Britain
	27 September: Tripartite Pact signed by Japan, Germany and Italy
1941	First use of Focke-Wulf 190 by Luftwaffe
	May: British seize German Enigma machine and code-book
	20 May: Germany invades Crete
	27 May: Sinking of German battleship *Bismarck*
	22 June: Germany invades Soviet Union in Operation Barbarossa
	9 October: Commencement of Manhattan Project approved by President Roosevelt
	7 December: Japan attacks Pearl Harbor
1942	OBOE (remote radar navigation system) introduced by RAF
	March: Start of heavy bombing campaign by RAF against Germany
	6–8 May: Battle of the Coral Sea
	4 June: Battle of Midway
	1 September–February 1943: Battle for Stalingrad
	23 October: Battle of El Alamein
1943	H2S (airborne radar navigation system) introduced by RAF
	WINDOW (anti-radar system) introduced by RAF
	July–August: Battle of Kursk
	10 July: Allies invade Sicily
1944	First use of Messerschmitt 262 jet aeroplane by Luftwaffe
	6 June: Allied invasion of Normandy coast in Operation Neptune (D-Day)
	12 June: First V-1s hit London
	8 September: First V-2s hit London
1945	10 March: USA drops 2000 tonnes of bombs on Tokyo
	April: Battle for Berlin
	7 May: Germany surrenders to Allies
	16 July: First atomic bomb tested (in New Mexico, USA)
	6 August: USA drops atomic bomb on Hiroshima
	9 August: USA drops atomic bomb on Nagasaki
	14 September: Japan agrees to unconditional surrender to Allies, ending World War Two
1949	Soviet Union tests its first atomic bomb

Further reading and places of interest

Further reading
Books
Non-fiction
History of Britain: The Blitz, Andrew Langley, Heinemann Library, 1995
Ultimate Aircraft, Philip Jarrett, Dorling Kindersley, 2000
World War II Aircraft, Jeffery L Ethell, Collins/Jane's, 1995
World War II Warships, Bernard Ireland, Collins/Jane's, 1999
Tanks: Look Inside: Cross-Sections, Richard Chasemore and Ian Harvey,
    Dorling-Kindersley, 1996
The Home Front: Women's War, Fiona Reynoldson, Wayland, 1991
The Home Front: Propaganda, Fiona Reynoldson, Wayland, 1991
Codes, Ciphers and Secret Writing, Martin Gardner, Dover Publications, 1985
Hiroshima: The Shadow of the Bomb, Richard Tames, Heinemann Library, 1999

Fiction
The Silver Sword, Ian Serraillier, Puffin Books, 1993
Carrie's War, Nina Bawden, Puffin Books, 2000
Echoes of War, Robert Westall, Puffin Books, 1995
The Machine Gunners, Robert Westall, Macmillan, 1994

Websites
World War Two encyclopedia site:
    www.spartacus.schoolnet.co.uk/2WW.htm
World War Two website:
    http://school.discovery.com/homeworkhelp/worldbook/atozhistory/w/610460.html
Website of the Imperial War Museum, London, a major repository of World War Two
    documents and artefacts:
    www.iwm.org.uk/

Places of interest
Imperial War Museum, London
HMS *Belfast* (World War Two cruiser), London
RAF Museum and American Air Museum, Duxford
Spitfire and Hurricane Memorial Building, RAF Manston, Kent
Kent Battle of Britain Museum, Hawkinge, Kent
Bovington Tank Museum, Dorset
Fleet Air Arm Museum, Yeovilton
Bletchley Park Trust (World War Two cipher centre), Milton Keynes

Glossary

ammunition bullets, shells, missiles, grenades and anything else fired during fighting

amphibious operating on land and in water

amplify increase the strength of a signal, such as a radio signal, or other noise

anti-bacterial able to kill bacteria

antibiotic medicine that fights infection

armour plating thick metal sheets to protect a tank or ship, for example, against shells and bullets

artillery large guns

ballistic missile guided long-range self-propelled missile

barrage barrier against an enemy action. An artillery barrage is a barrier of heavy shellfire used to cover one's own side in an attack or defend against an enemy attack.

barrel tube of a gun through which ammunition is fired

bayonet metal blade attached to a gun

casualty wounded or killed person

caterpillar track revolving steel band, made up of joined sections, that is used instead of wheels for vehicles that travel on rough ground or in mud

civilian citizen of a country who is not in the armed forces

commando soldier trained to carry out operations behind enemy lines

convoy group of ships travelling together with an armed escort

cryptanalyst specialist in devising and breaking codes

detonate make something explode

dive-bomber aircraft that releases its bombs while diving towards its target

electromechanical using electricity to operate switches and other parts

electronic relating to electrons, the basic particles of electricity, and used to describe devices using electronic power

element one of about 100 simple substances that make up all other substances

empire territory, usually covering more than one country or area, ruled by an emperor or other supreme ruler

epidemic disease spreading rapidly and affecting many people at once

evacuate get people out of a particular area in an emergency situation

firestorm unstoppable blaze sometimes produced when air is sucked into an area set on fire by bombs

flak exploding anti-aircraft shells. From the German for anti-aircraft defence.

front line the foremost section of an army's defended territory and the most exposed to the enemy

fuse device that sets off an explosion

genocide systematic destruction of a national, racial or religious group

glider aeroplane without an engine

grenade small explosive device either thrown by hand or fired from a launcher

guided missile weapon that travels through the air or water directed by remote control

home front situation or contributions of civilians in a nation at war

howitzer type of gun which fires shells on a high trajectory

incendiary bomb bomb designed to set fire to buildings or other targets

infantry soldiers who fight on foot

innovation something new or changed

insecticide chemical that kills insects

jam block or confuse radio signals so they become unreadable

laser device for producing a beam of light capable of travelling vast distances

manoeuvrable easy to move, turn or control in other ways

offensive used for attacking. Also means a large pre-planned attack.

periscope instrument with which a person can observe from a concealed position, such as from a submerged submarine or over the top of a wall

piston engine engine using a piston and piston-rod. The piston is a disc or cylinder that moves up and down inside a tube to create motion.

quinine anti-malarial drug extracted from the bark of a tropical tree

radar system that detects and locates objects by bouncing radio waves off them

radiation sending out of rays, especially used to refer to large amounts of rays harmful to people

radiation sickness damage to body tissue resulting from exposure to nuclear radiation

recoil spring back after being fired

reconnaissance military observation to assess an enemy's strength and movement

reinforcements extra support, such as new men or weapons brought into a battle

rifle long-barrelled firearm which has a rifled (spirally grooved) barrel. This spins the bullet being fired, to give it both longer range and greater accuracy.

rocket projectile that carries its own oxygen supply to burn fuel

round bullet and cartridge. The cartridge contains an explosive charge to propel the bullet from the gun, and is ejected once the bullet has been fired.

shells metal cases of various shapes containing explosives or other harmful materials

sonar (short for sound navigation and ranging) system that detects and locates objects underwater through the use of soundwaves

stalemate situation where both sides in a conflict are unable to defeat each other

strategy overall plan for dealing with a conflict or a battle

strongpoint defensive position on battlefront that has extra fortifications or weapons

supersonic faster than the speed of sound

technology knowledge and ability that improves ways of doing practical things

telegraph device for sending messages along wires

trajectory path taken by an object as it flies through the air

transfusion injection of blood into a wounded person to replace blood lost in an injury

turret small tower on a tank or ship that holds and protects guns and gunners.

vacuum tube tube from which air has been removed that was used as an amplifier in early electronic devices

velocity speed of an object's movement

warhead the part of a missile containing an explosive charge

Index